D1186591

THE
ALTERNATIVE
GARDENER

THE
ALTERNATIVE
GARDENER

A COMPOST OF QUIPS FOR
THE GREEN-FINGERED

William Rushton

GRAFTON BOOKS

A Division of the Collins Publishing Group

LONDON GLASGOW
TORONTO SYDNEY AUCKLAND

Grafton Books
A Division of the Collins Publishing Group
8 Grafton Street, London W1X 3LA

Published by Grafton Books 1986

British Library Cataloguing in Publication Data

Rushton, William
   The alternative gardener : a compost of quips
   for the green-fingered.
   1. Gardening – Anecdotes, facetiae, satire, etc.
   I. Title
   635'.0207   SB455

ISBN 0–246–12734–1

Printed in Great Britain by
William Collins Sons & Co Ltd, Great Britain

CONTENTS

The answer lies in the toil

THE
ALTERNATIVE
GARDENER

1 GARDENING – THE WHYS AND WHY NOTS

What makes a man wish to become a gardener?

Is it the love of wildlife? A liking for plants? A hatred for Thripp? A feeling that whatever Mother Nature can do – he can do better?

No – few gardeners garden for the love of the garden. Most positively detest the sight of it. What then persuades a man to exchange the warmth and comfort of his hearth for the Passchendaele of the garden?

Your immediate answer may be – the Little Woman. And has it ever occurred to you that, had Adolf Hitler changed sex suddenly and violently in 1943 – he would have been a Little Woman? No, this is sexist talk and unworthy of any gardener.

1. THE RECLUSIVE GARDENER By far the greatest number of gardeners are evacuees who have sought sanctuary

and solitude in the garden. The potting shed or greenhouse is their Total Exclusion Zone from which they can plot their manoeuvres – an island of peace in an increasingly rowdy world. These men (who are rarely women) are refugee gardeners who have exchanged physical comfort for emotional comfort in the cold outdoors. You will recognise them at once by the calm, uncluttered look of those who have found inner peace of mind. Their considered step and reluctance to return indoors even in the harshest of conditions immediately set them apart.

2. THE SOCIAL GARDENER He gardens because socially it is expected of him by neighbours and relations. He resents the need to spend time and money on the garden, but is not prepared to risk social censure by refusing to conform. Like a car, the garden is an extension of his social standing and, also like the car, it must be replaced at regular intervals and at ever greater cost. This man will barely know the garden he creates except by its cost. Ask him the names of the plants he has purchased and he will be hard pressed to name one. But ask him the exact cost and chances are he will be able to pin a price-tag to every last shoot. (He may well have never removed it.) The social gardener will arrange his garden to look

outward, not inward: beds will be arranged to face the public thoroughfare where they can be appreciated by envious neighbours and the front garden will naturally demand more attention than the rear.

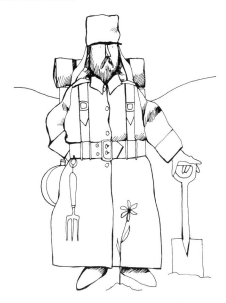

3. THE REAL GARDENER A man who seems, at least on the surface, to gain pleasure from his gardening. He will dwell lovingly on the merits of seed stock, will consider and tend his garden with meticulous care and enthusiasm. On the surface he will seem content – but this is not a happy man. His deep love for gardening belies some tragedy in his life: a lost love, a found love, an ambition that has failed, a deep-rooted desire that may never now be realised. This man is using his garden as a crutch (see AILMENTS – Gardener's Crutch), on which to lean to hide his despair at some lost dream, some ambition unfulfilled. Look into his eyes – they are not the eyes of a man at ease with himself, they are the eyes of an incomplete man, of sadness, of loss. A man who, in the past, might well have joined the French Foreign Legion and spent forlorn years watering the desert.

4. THE NATURIST This man believes that by cultivating his small square of Mother Earth he is in some way giving back to nature that which he has taken out. He sees gardening as a crusade, a debt that it is his duty to repay. He is never sure what the debt is actually for, only that it must be paid by a lifetime's penance. By caring and tending for his plants he believes that Mother Nature will be aided and improved. The folly of his ways is clear to see. The most natural, most environmentally conscious thing for anybody to do is to leave Mother Nature to herself, to allow *her* to decide the best uses for the sod and soil.

She needs no help, no encouragement. If ever there was an act opposed to nature, it was turning the land into a manicured and patchwork quilt of hybrid flowers. The Naturist is fooling only himself. Alas, he is unlikely to change his ways.

5. THE PURGALIST His use of the garden is based on his own belief that he should pay some sort of mythical debt to society. By purging himself with a life in which every waking hour is spent in the garden in the most tedious and back-breaking positions, he somehow believes that he will emerge a better man. He can be easily identified by his deliberation in selecting only the most shattering and tiring jobs going. He will make a deliberate point of standing in the most awkward posture, or stooping in the most painful way. Not for him the Radox bath – only the short sharp shock of the cold shower; from it all he intends to emerge, somehow, a better man.

6. THE GULLIBLIST He has been led to believe, by a combination of books and television programmes, that it is possible for man to provide much of the sustenance he needs simply from his own back yard. Glibly accepting that it should be possible with only a little light work to out-manoeuvre the entire horticultural trade and provide cheap, nourishing produce, he spends hundreds of hours tending a few handfuls

of vegetables that, had he bought them in the shops, would have cost a few pence. It is a common error to believe that amateurs can undercut the professionals. Were we able to produce at a time when the rest of the producers were unable to, we might be on to something. As it is, most home-grown produce appears at just that moment when the marketplace heaves beneath a glut. For the time and money amateur gardeners spend growing their own supplies, they could have bought out the entire horticultural trade three times over. However, the Gulliblist hangs grimly on to his determination to succeed and refuses to accept the reasoned arguments against him. Self-help also causes blindness and stunted growth.

7. THE FADDIST This man is not a gardener at all. Six months ago he had never set foot in a garden. In six months' time he will wish he never had. He is born of a generation that devours any new pastime or craze before the rest of us have realised it has arrived. He has delved into every hobby going and has lasted about as long at each. Observe his thirst for knowledge (however trivial), the books and magazines that fuel his enthusiasm. He is not a true gardener; his zeal will soon wilt and his expensive gardening tools be traded in for a camera, Compact Disc player or home computer.

A potted history of gardens

The history of gardening begins very early in the history of man, perhaps before 2000 B.C. (*Before Cheeseplants*). Paintings of men pruning fruit trees, watering, using sickles, arranging pot plants, and using the lawnmower (ATCO: Ego Lottus Lessus Bovvus Sum Quam Hovvus) are now known in the early European cultures.

At the same time, in India and Persia, many sweet-scented flowers, especially roses, were cultivated by rulers who made fine gardens as a setting for their palaces and temples (see chapter on Indian Gardening, not in this book but try *Kama into the Sutra, Maud*; also see *The Perfumed Gardener* – Lord Lawn-porn).

Chinese gardens began before 2000 B.C. (see chapter on 2000 B.C., not in this book either or in *Come into the Garden, Mao*), and were very popular, especially in China where most of them were. Marco Polo (the thirteenth-century Venetian traveller – not to be confused with Marc O'Polo, the Irish landscape gardener and demolition contractor with a hole in his head (see different chapter in different book entirely)) brought many flowers and shrubs back to England (see chapter on England, in this book originally but since removed). Polo's successors (don't see Chapter on Polo, Water, not in this book but in other books, which is completely irrelevant and is a game played without horses; see Polo, Ordinary, a sort of mounted golf popular with Prince Charles, but not with his lady wife) brought back flowers and shrubs and trees to Europe in the eighteenth and nineteenth centuries. Characteristic Chinese garden designs were based on miniature reproductions of natural landscapes and were not merely faithful copies of real landscapes; each twig and stone had some symbolic meaning (see *Twigs And How To Understand Them*).

EUROPEAN GARDENS Gardens flourished first in the Roman Empire. Cicero, Plutarch and Pliny wrote accounts of gardens (see chapters in this book, since removed though subsequently re-inserted before being finally removed again) which included marble pools, colonnades, pergolas, cornettos, zavaronis, platinis, wombles, cypress groves, rose gardens, flower beds, camp beds, orchards, vineyards, myrtles, olives, Laurel groves and Hardy annuals (but no gnomes).

I HAVE JUST TURNED WINE INTO INSECTICIDE

In the Middle Ages, gardens were kept by monks who cultivated farms, orchards and gardens around monasteries (hence the derivation of the Cistercian order who took their name from the Nasturtium that flowered against their abbey walls). Monks also invented Football, Chanel No. 5, green sticky drinks that make you fall over and Silence.

Italian gardeners carried on the work of the monks in the fourteenth and fifteenth centuries – cascades, grottoes, terraces, garden theatres, tall trees and etc. (see etc.), and produced extremely fine gardens. This was often called the Age of Renaissance Gardening because that's what it was called, so just mind your own business.

FRENCH GARDENS Le Nôtre (1613–1700) dominated French gardening. The 'grand' gardens he built to suit the grand houses of the period were larger than anything seen before. Water, parterres and orangeries were used to create a landscape of formal tradition. The whole work was carried on after Le Nôtre's death from a surfeit of cheese by his wife, Mrs Le Nôtre, or Le Nôtre Dame as she preferred to be called. Le Nôtre was one of the most powerful men in France at the time – which either says a great deal about him or not a lot about France. (Discuss.)

ENGLISH GARDENS The Tudors were the first to lay out gardens in response to Tudor Court life, and Hampton Court Maze is a fine example of these early gardens. Topiary became very popular during this period ('Topiary Is The Popular One' became abbreviated to the more common phrase 'Top is the Pop's', or 'Tope Of The Popes') and many fine houses were surrounded by a wall of topiary figures (see entirely different chapter in a book not yet published but I imagine you're all looking forward to it with a keen sense of anticipation). During the seventeenth century, many foreign plants came to Britain; in Oxford, botanical gardens were laid out. Le Nôtre's pupils were regular visitors to England during this period and designed gardens and parks in the French manner, a practice that continued until the eighteenth century when the Romantic Movement took over.

Painters and poets now sought to naturalise and colour the landscape; they despised the work of Le Nôtre, which wasn't surprising as basically he was a froggie and no one likes a smart-arsed frog. Garden walls disappeared, then trees, then

paths. In fact before long everything disappeared, only to reappear again in a completely different order, thanks to the landscape gardener. Indeed the passion for 'landscaping' spread as far as France where 'Le Jardin à l'Anglais' (literally: 'the garden that is one in the eye for you frogs') became fashionable.

At the beginning of the twentieth century, notable gardeners such as William Robinson and Gertrude Jekyll brought back hardy flowering plants (often and quite rightly confused with 'hardly flowering plants') to break down the uninspired Victorian garden (and also the uninspired Victorian gardener who spent most of his time in the woodshed seducing titled ladies and appearing in romantic novels of the period). Since then the development of the small garden has been predominant. Oh yes, and Enter Left – the gnome.

FERTILISER

The seven ages of gardening man

The youngest of the gardening ages is that of youth, stretching from one's late thirties, when man first becomes interested in gardening, to the early sixties. During this period the gardener is young(ish), keen(ish) and quite possibly, apart from this, a normal human being.

The second age begins in the early sixties. The gardener now has more time on his hands. He therefore does far less work. Often he will do nothing at all. This is the age of maturity.

The third age of gardening begins in the early seventies. The gardener will sit for long periods and reflect. He has time to collect his thoughts. In fact, by the time he has collected them there is often no time left for anything else.

The fourth age of gardening begins in the early eighties. The gardener now has time to collect together any thoughts he didn't have time to collect together previously. He will also have time to re-collect those thoughts he had collected once before but has now forgotten. He won't have time for gardening. He will be wrestling with his great book – *The Collected Thoughts of an 80-Year-Old Gardener.*

The fifth age of gardening (see the fourth age of gardening).

The sixth age of gardening (see the fifth age of gardening).

The seventh age of gardening. In this age the gardener is at the twilight of his gardening career. He collects his thoughts together for one last time ... then dies ... though not always in that order.

Lilies

Do's and don'ts of gardening

Do   buy a house with no garden.

Don't   worry when the man from three doors away calls and asks if you want your garden back, as it is crawling over his fence.

Don't   be embarrassed if you borrow next door's lawnmower and lose it in the grass.

Don't   be afraid to ask for your greenhouse back when it collapses through next door's fence.

Don't   let neighbours upset you when your creeping ivy creeps next door and attempts a half-Nelson on their house.

Don't   be alarmed if your garden receives a visit from an expert at the School of Tropical Diseases.

Don't   be concerned if he tells you there is a tiger loose in the undergrowth.

Don't   assume that gardening is about gardens.

Do   assume that gardening is all about social standing.

It is as well to remember that gardens are as much a barometer of your status as the type of car you drive. But don't forget that only those who conform can take part. Anyone who allows his garden to fall into neglect and disuse is disqualified.

Those who *do* take part in the gardening stakes immediately set themselves upon the rungs of the competitive ladder. Those who *don't* sensibly set themselves apart from the scramble. Once you make an effort to let your garden go to ruin you immediately slither down the snake – and remember where that put in its first appearance.

A neglected garden immediately poses imponderable questions. Why are you doing it? Are you barking mad or simply eccentric? Are you one of those reclusive millionaires one reads about in the papers who wear empty Kleenex boxes on their feet and leave all their money to the cats' home? Do you have a title?

Cherish the image your flaccid idleness creates. Allow the garden to run wild with abandon. Buy a Ford Popular. By curious perversity, you may in fact set off again up the social ladder you had intended to step off, simply by your own inactivity. The less you do, the greater the air of mystery you create. The greater the mystery you create, the higher your social standing may rise. Dropping out can be as effective as dropping Names. Or indeed dropping Gnomes.

Other tips

- Arrange for strange visitors to arrive at the house at odd hours of the night or day.
- Do not possess a television.
- Pay for all you buy in cash.
- Write repeatedly to the palace. The palace replies to all mail sent; the distinctively headed envelopes that arrive (with the help of a talkative postman) will immediately cause gossip to run rife.
- Arrive home in the middle of the week with large suitcases.

Remember: these hints apply principally to estate-plan houses in smaller towns. In isolated villages or inner-city areas, eccentrics are less likely to draw attention to themselves. In the latter case, the answer is to get on 'Pebble Mill At One' or one of those television programmes that like to drag odd-balls out from under their stone whenever they have nothing better to do.

Common ailments suffered by the gardener

GALLOPING HOUSEPLANTS The debilitating disease in which the gardener loses the tenure of his house to houseplants. Early symptoms: loss of cats, dogs, television set, wife, children.

GARDENITIS GARDENITIS An extreme form of *Green Finger* (see below) in which the eyes also turn green when faced with a fellow gardener's prize blooms.

'GREEN TUMMY' is a gardeners' disease often associated with excessive prune eating.

GOOSE GREEN A sharp sensation enjoyed by gardeners when crouching.

GREEN ALL OVER Associated with road traffic safety and not a gardening disease at all.

POTTER'S POT An unpleasant irritation causing the victim constantly to remove plants from one pot to another for no apparent reason. Generally results in the plant concerned eventually dying and the process recommencing with a new plant.

WEEDER'S WEED Uncontrollable affliction in which a compulsive weeder finds it impossible to stop weeding (hence the phrase, 'I can't give up the dreaded weed'). Weeders with Weeder's Weed suffer terrible withdrawal symptoms if they are stopped from weeding and may eventually wilt. Or tear the Wilton to pieces.

INGROWING GREENHOUSE Common illness in which plants within the greenhouse grow inwards and eventually prevent the gardener himself from actually entering. Associated with *Galloping Houseplants* (see above).

ACUTE PATIO A prolonged disease in which the gardener suffers from diminished garden as a result of covering the entire surface area with a patio. (Often associated with *Gardenae Furnito*, in which more and more indoor and outdoor space is given over to the display of garden furniture. A disease first introduced into this country by garden centres.)

GNOMES DISEASE A disease of the front garden in which large areas of the frontal aspects become infected with gnomes

and garden-pot furniture. Cases can be treated with 'caustic remarks', but more severe forms of infestation have proved to be immune and may need to be removed by special hand-picked teams of men disguised as drunken football supporters who are trained to enter gardens and kick the heads off malignant gnomes.

MOWERS' SYNDROME Occurs when lawnmower owners feel compelled to buy new lawnmowers despite the fact that the previous one still performs perfectly well. Sufferers from Mowers' Syndrome may find they have five or six lawnmowers blocking the shed floor and that they are increasingly difficult to remove when required. Often associated with *Hovers Syndrome*, a disease of the brain which causes prominent lawnmower manufacturers to take part in increasingly extravagant and pointless advertising stunts.

GREEN FINGER Common name given to the disease *Greenus fungus*.

PURPLE FINGER Common name for *Erectus Fencus Finger*.

RED FINGER See *Mowers' Syndrome*. A symptomatic disease affecting lawnmower and power operatives.

NO FINGER An extreme form of *Red Finger*.

FLUORESCENT FINGER Often called Crop Sprayer's Revenge.

GARDEN POX A type of Herbes suffered by regular growers of herbs (*Greenus Penis*).

SHINGLES An unpleasant infection that causes the gardener to fill the boot of his car with enormous quantities of small stones after seaside holidays with the idea of using them to infill a gravel drive, only for the clutch, transmission and rear-end axle to be completely ruined on the journey home.

Cycles of nature

Remember that nature is a cycle. Anything that you do to it will always come back to haunt you!

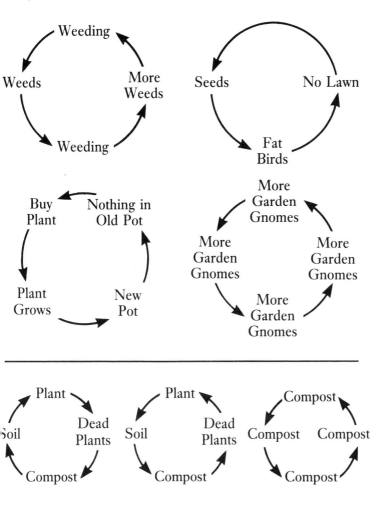

CORRECT   INCORRECT   COMPOST
                                    MANUFACTURER

Gardenomics

Gardenomics: the science of measuring one's gardenility (susceptibility to gardening books).

1. Do you become clammy and wet when fingering fresh seed catalogues?
   YES/NO/A BIT (OH, ALL RIGHT, YES)

2. Do you feel a bond of friendship with shrubbery?
   YES/YES/YES AND NO/YES/OTHER (Please specify)

3. Would you rather spend the evening with an attractive woman or an attractive houseplant?
   YES/NO/ARSENAL

4. Do you find leafmould stimulating?
   YES/A BIT/A BIT MORE THAN A BIT/A LOT

5. Do you think leafmould finds you stimulating?
   YES/YES/YES/YES/YES/YES/OTHER (See YES)

6. Would you risk your life for a bag of potting compost?
   NO/NO/NO/NO/YES/JOANNA LUMLEY

7. Have you ever had fun with a rotavator?
   NO/YES/YES, AND THE HOSPITAL DID AN AMAZING JOB

8. Would you be prepared to share your life with a pond weed?
   YES

9. How would you describe your relationship with plants?
   LOVING/CARING/SHARING/DEVOTED/PURELY PLUTONIC/SIZZLING

10. Would you ever leave your husband/wife because of your garden?

    MAYBE/PROBABLY/POSSIBLY/EITHER YES OR NO/I ALREADY HAVE

11. Would your husband/wife ever leave you because of their garden?

    1963/OFFSIDE/LEICESTER CITY/ PETER SHILTON/THE FIFTH ROUND/ SELINA SCOTT

12. Do you hang around garden centres dressed as a plant?

    YES/NO/WHY?/NAME NAMES

The Toulouse-Lautrec scarecrow

2 THE LORE OF GARDENING

For many years the gardener has provided the world with the best in earth-bred philosophy. Rich in flavour, rich in text, rich in language, rich in understanding of the sod and soil. And above all, rich in uselessness.

How to become a gardening folkel (a gardening yokel who tells folk tales):

You will need:

(a) trousers with crutch below the knee
(b) jumper with four sleeve holes
(c) jacket that used to be a dishcloth
(d) between $2\frac{1}{2}$ and $3\frac{1}{2}$ teeth
(e) a chin with over 3 inches of fresh stubble
(f) wood-burning clay pipe
(g) wood-burning clay underpants
(h) socks that not only breathe but actually snore
      when you take them off
(i) secondhand hair
(j) a threadbare sheep dog with between $2\frac{1}{2}$ and $3\frac{1}{2}$ legs
(k) string tied below the knees.

You should:

(a) sit on a five-bar gate
(b) sit on a five-bar fire (check with wood-burning
      underpants first)
(c) cogitate
(d) ruminate
(e) masticate
(f) pick your nose
(g) pick somebody else's nose
(h) pick your teeth
(i) offer your teeth to somebody else for them
      to pick
(j) put your teeth back in horse's mouth.

And before replying to any question you should:

(a) sigh
(b) whistle through teeth
(c) whistle through tooth
(d) whistle through mouth
(e) whistle through other
      mouth
(f) shake your head
(g) shake everything but your
      mouth
(h) light your clay pipe
(i) light your clay underpants
(j) ask for money.

How to construct a good homily

A Good Homily will contain information:

... Your garden will do well ...
... your garden will not do well ...
... your garden is about to turn into a frog ...
... your garden is about to turn into a motorway
     intersection ...

*This information will depend on some forthcoming act of nature, for
example:*

... if the lark rises early ...
... if the lark rises late ...
... if the lark doesn't rise at all ...
... if the hollyberry rises early ...
... if the hollyberry blossoms late ...
... if the winter/summer/spring/autumn be wet/dry/
     large/dribbly ...
... if the hollyberry/lark/Jack Frost be wet/dry/tall/
     thin/wobbly ...

Thus:

Them do say	that if lark rises early
Some do say	if lark rises late
It be said	if lark doesn't rise at all
Certain as most	if hollyberry rises early
True as nigh	if hollyberry blossoms late
Be it known	if the winter/summer/spring/autumn/ be wet/dry/large/dribbly
	if the hollyberry/lark/Jack Frost be wet/dry/tall/thin/wobbly

A second clause will be added:

    ... and the Horn of Plenty ...
    ... and the Hawthorn Berry ...
    ... and the cowmaid's pretty knickers ...

And qualified:

    ... be damp
    ... be long
    ... be merry
    ... be sticky
    ... be silent
    ... be bop a looba
    ... be movie

The whole will be prefaced by an old adage:

    Them do say ...
    Some do say ...
    It be said ...
    Certain as most ...
    True as nigh ...
    Be it known ...

the Horn of Plenty
the Hawthorn Berry
the cowmaid's pretty
ickers
	be damp
	be long
	be merry
	be sticky
	be silent
	be bop a looba
	be movie
		then your garden
		  will do well
		then your garden
		  will not do well
		then your garden
		  is about to turn
		  into a frog
		then your garden
		  is about to turn
		  into a motorway
		  intersection

Phrase and fable of the gardener

Where ne'erdowell and honeysuckle do rankle, snowbursts may a plenty grow.

LITERALLY: It will be cold in the north, but later in the day a trough of low pressure will cover much of Britain, bringing occasional light rain.

The sun blows hard, blow ye clouds that September ripens.

LITERALLY: Squally showers over England, Scotland, Ireland and North Wales. Watch out for fog inland.

When wind to swell my bumstead hay, I will dangle with the foxgloves in the golden crocus pond at dawn.

UNLITERALLY: My car has broken down, is there a public telephone in the vicinity?

When tuft and curd meet willows leet what heeds the ploughman's curse.

LITERALLY: You have an appealing body, would you direct me to the nearest omnibus depot that I might arrange transport.

When green fills mudlarks' clammy fingers the golden ochre of summer's shafts brings the honeysuckle forth.

SOMEWHAT UNLITERALLY: nik nokki nik nok
                      nikki nakki noo
                      nik nokki nik nok
                      to you

The heather burdens another pinch with budding flower but where dwells the heather that was tomorrow's sunny dawn?

VERY LITERALLY: The heather burdens another pinch with budding flower but where dwells the heather that was tomorrow's sunny dawn?

When plumpkin he do sway his gentle head I will lead a daisy that he springs summer eternal.

LITERALLY: I am an attractive 26-year-old divorcee with vivacious pouting lips and would like to meet a fun-loving gent for life, love, and extremely heavy petting sessions.

As the larkin birds mildew rests, the hearts of the heavy morrow kisses broadbean honeysuckle good day milking.

LITERALLY: My trousers are rather hot, please remove them before my buttocks catch fire, you gorgeous heaving beauty, you.

Wild bee brings the honey to the croft, but who treads the summer pondweed that chaffs the early cludd?

SOMEWHAT LITERALLY: 1965 Ford Anglia for sale. One careful lady stunt driver from new. £25,000 o.n.o. No Bishops this time, please. Also half-eaten piece of toast for sale. Would consider swap for similar in gold and orange.

As season greets the turning day will winter's crowning glory sit proud on the silver light of wheat.

LITERALLY: Hello, I'm conducting a survey into loft insulation in your area and I wondered if I could ask you a few simple questions.

May your camels prosper and mate incessantly, may they bear fruit in great profusion, but not in your living-room.

LITERALLY: Hello, I've come to read your meter.

Talking to plants

When talking to your plants, the use of the following Internationally Recognised Phrases is recommended:

I would like you to propagate immediately.
May I fertilise your root?
I must de-infest your shrubbery immediately.
I wish to take a cutting, do not wilt.
Would you like to go outside and extend your foliage?
I will re-pot your clippings immediately
I see you have a large trunk; would you like me to prune it?
I will not dust your succulents now; they look withered.

May I have the pleasure of covering your tendrils with leaf
     mould?
What's a nice bedding plant like you doing in a place like this?

Phrases not to use when speaking to plants:
Grow, you bastard!
If you don't flower I'll kill you, greeny!
Stuff you, Jimmy.

3 THE GARDENING YEAR

January

The foxglove proud, erect, stern and fierce
A lot less erect if you tread on it!

JANUARY

1 Nothing
2 Nothing very much
3 Very little
4 Even less
5 Plant sweet f.a.
6 Water sweet f.a.
7 Weed sweet f.a.
8 Rest
9 More rest
10 More nothing
11 Nothing again
12 Even more nothing than nothing
13 Very little again
14 Ditto
15 Ditto
16 Ditto
17 Ditto (see above)
18 Further ditto (see above and below)
19 Even further ditto
20 Don't cut down overgrown shrubs today
21 Don't fork over soil today
22 Don't whatever you do place dahlias in boxes and cover over with light soil
23 Nothing
24 Extremely very little
25 Plant sweet buggerall
26 Nothing much today either
27 No, not much today as well
28 The same as yesterday (or less)
29 Rest
30 More rest
31 Extremely nothing

February

Crab apple tree its blossom fair
In milky silken glen,
The parsnip and the blackthorn bush,
the holly and the pear;
the rosehip and the hornbeam,
the bayleaf crisp and fresh ...
Bother, I had the last two lines written down
And I've forgotten them!

FEBRUARY

1 Don't raise a finger to everlasting flowers
2 Look at wellingtons
3 Look at Rose Acroclinium and Rhodanthe
4 Look at sky
5 Look at sky again
6 Ignore weeding strawberries completely
7 Ignore early peas and broad beans
8 Ignore everything else you haven't already ignored
9 Nail bird-table in position
10 Nail bird-table in position for second time, remove nail from dead bird inside
11 Kill anything still living in garden
12 Kill anything not still living in garden
13 Sprain ankle
14 Rest
15 Rest
16 See above
17 See below
18 Rest
19 Rest (see Rest)
20 Convalesce (see rest)
21 Ditto
22 Further ditto
23 Light exercise (see Rest)
24 Light rest (see exercise)
25 Forking sweet f.a.
26 Sweet forking f.a.
27 Forking sweet forking f.a.
28 The forking same

March

A rose that bursts full colour
Its rich and cherished leaf
Its colour and its fragrance . . .
Damn I've pricked my bloody self with it!

MARCH

1 Trim ivy from walls of house by affixing to car bumper and pulling forward smartly
2 Remove a weed
3 Plant something
4 Plant something else
5 Drop paving slab on foot
6 Rest
7 Rest
8 Rest
9 Rest of rest
10 Take a rest from resting
11 Remove another weed (optional)
12 Rest
13 Try to remember where you left greenhouse
14 Rest
15 Contemplate planting out layered carnations
16 Contemplate planting out new fruit trees
17 Give consideration to sowing early carrots
18 Ruminate upon the possibilities of ventilating cold frames
19 Cogitate on the first planting of gladioli
20 Think deeply about placing manure around new fruit trees
21 Dwell learnedly on the opportunities for repotting
22 Brood sensibly on the need to pinch out chrysanthemum tips
23 Ponder replanting herbs
24 Dwell upon the need to lime soil for pea crop
25 Rest
26 Further rest
27 A spot of light weeding perhaps
28 Rest
29 Rest
30 Rest
31 Toss a few seeds about

April

The Elder flower
Soft crimson pink
Dew burst on April morn;
Fresh marigold
Springs forth in bloom
Oh, what a load of drivel

APRIL

1 Sow hardy annuals where they are blown (not essential)
2 Transplant seedlings of half-hardy annuals in boxes (optional)
3 Finish all planting and division of herbaceous plants (ignore)
4 Hardy lilies may now be planted (if you feel up to it)
5 Plant tubers in boxes to start growth (not absolutely vital)
6 Sow annual fragrants near the house (could possibly ignore, too)
7 Dig something
8 Plant something
9 Weed something
10 Tie up something (or other)
11 Spray something (or other)
12 Tread on something important
13 Sit on something
14 Water something
15 Break something
16 Something
17 Something else
18 Rest
19 Protect seeds from birds by shooting birds
20 Thin out hardy annuals by walking across them
21 Develop sudden allergy to all plants
22 Nothing
23 Nothing
24 Nothing
25 Earth up early potatoes and throw them away
26 Have another look for greenhouse
27 Throw out all old houseplants and buy a new set
28 See above (or below) (but not both)
29 See below (or across) (but not above)
30 See above and below (at the same time) (but not across)

May

My garden is like a May shower
Plip Plop Plip Plop Plip Plop
Plip Plop Plip Plop Plip Plop
Plip Plop Plip Plop Plip Plop
Plip Plop Plip Plop Plip Plop
Plip Plop Plip Plop Plip Plop
Plop

. . . Plip!

(only without so many Plip Plops)

MAY

1	3	5	4	7	9	8
6	2	10	20	12	19	13
11	18	17	14	16	15	29
23	28	21	24	22	26	25
27	30	31	29	34	32	33
35	37	36	40	39	57	

(Rearrange these dates into
correct order and do nothing on
any of them)

Haute-Couture scarecrow

June

My garden grows in summer
My garden grows in spring;
That's why my garden's covered
In creepy crawly things.

JUNE

1	2	3	4	5	6	7
8	9	10	11	12	13	14
15	16	17	18	19	20	21
22	23	24	25	26	27	28
29	30	[31]				

(Days when gardening should
take place marked thus ☐)

July

My garden is in flower now
A thousand different shades
Exciting and enchanting now
And what a bloody pain!

JULY

*SPECIAL NOTE TO
GARDENERS:*

ALL GARDENING
CANCELLED FOR MONTH
OF JULY OWING TO
CIRCUMSTANCES AND
PLANTS BEYOND
CONTROL.

August

De dum de dee
De dum de dee
Dum dee dee dum dee dee
dee dee dee dum
dee dee dee dum
et cetera et cetera

AUGUST

1	Plants need all the light and air they can get at this time of year. Don't go near them or you might deprive them
2	Go on holiday
3–21	Holiday
22–31	Holiday

September

Fair blows the wind
That churls the bough
And aches in weary spinney . . .
I just wrote that, and now I feel
A really silly ninny.

SEPTEMBER

Tips for gardeners this month: *Don't!*

Robert Maxwell
look-alike scare

October

The Larch The Pine The Fir The Oak
The Sycamore The Elm
If I had a bulldozer
I'd kill the bloody lot

OCTOBER

*NOTICE TO ALL
GARDENERS ... WARNING!*

The risk of fog during much of
October makes gardening
extremely hazardous. Even in a
small garden the gardener may
be lost for days wandering
around aimlessly, unable to get
back to the house. Wear bright
clothing, carry a torch, arm
yourself with flares and
searchlights and don't forget a
whistle. Follow these
instructions and, above all, stay
indoors whenever possible.

November

Ode To Winter

Winter's here
Frost is sharp
Ice white upon the water
Crisp and firm
November air
Thick pair of woolly knickers

NOVEMBER

1   Notoriously bad day for all gardeners
2   Even more notoriously bad day for gardeners
3   Perhaps the most notoriously bad day for gardening in the whole year
4   After this one
5   Useful opportunity to blow up as much of the garden as possible
6   Cut back any remaining chrysanthemums
7   Extinguish still-smouldering honeysuckle
8   Notoriously good day for not gardening
9   Notoriously good day for doing the same as yesterday
10 Notoriously good day for doing the same as tomorrow
11 Notoriously good day for doing the same as yesterday
12 Lilies of the Valley are best left till spring
13 Currants and gooseberries are best left till summer
14 Everything else is simply best left
15 Remember, the more you plant now the more you will have to harvest later in the year
16 Catch a cold
17 Stay indoors and keep warm
18 Don't prune bean poles
19 Don't mow cat
20 Don't water goldfish
21 Catch another cold
22 Catch another cold
23 Catch the same cold you caught only a week ago again
24 Don't do anything
25 Do even less
26 Notoriously good day for filling in your football pools coupon all day
27 Notorious day for catching colds and staying indoors
28 Weed the cat
29 Weed the gnomes
30 Catch another cold

December

My garden is a little ship
That's tossed around at sea
But there is one can't give a toss –
You've guessed! That's right, it's me.

DECEMBER

1 Something that involves being warm

2 Something that involves not being cold

3 Something that involves not going outside

4 Something that involves the television

5 Something that involves the pub

6 Something that doesn't involve the word 'gardening'

7 Something that involves a chair

8 Something that involves snoring

9 Something that involves an object with blankets and sheets

10 Something that involves something with a dartboard and snug

11 Something that involves something like the something above

12 Something (or other) (but not cold)

13 Something or other that involves the phrase 'no gardening today'

14 Something with the word 'indoors'

15 Buy the Christmas tree (artificial)

16 Ignore plants displaced by frost

17 Ignore (insert as appropriate)

18 Ignore (   ) (insert as appropriate)

19 Ignore (   ) (insert as appropriate)

20 Ignore (   ), (   ) and (   ) (insert as appropriate)

21 (   ) (insert as required)

22 (   ) (   ) with a (   ) (insert as required)

23 see 16th–22nd inclusive

24 Christmas Eve – officially a non-garden day

25 Christmas Day – well, be honest, you're not going to do anything today, are you?

26 Or today?

27 Probably nothing today either

28 Leave it till tomorrow

29 Leave it till tomorrow

30 Leave it till tomorrow

31 Leave it till next year

4 THOUGHT FOR FOOD

The gardener as provider

While the average gardener can, with some effort, be persuaded to cultivate produce that is fit to eat, rarely will such produce make a contribution to the dinner table that will amount to more than an acute case of financial suicide when all energies are costed in. Indeed, even the most zealous gardener can hardly hope to compete with the professional cultivator when the costs of his own labours are taken into account.

Assessing this ludicrous state of affairs is not always as easy as it might seem. None of us shares a common price for our labour, and if we take the cost of employing some other person to work our gardens for us, then we deny the very principle upon which home gardeners work, namely self-sufficiency.

By way of illustration, take the case of a well-paid corporate official – say, a banker or lawyer. Count up the hours he spends in weeding; it is quite likely that in terms of labour alone the average cauliflower dug from his soil will cost somewhere in the region of forty to fifty pounds . . . more, if the soil is difficult to turn or requires frequent attention.

Of course, it is generally assumed that this cost is partly offset by the pleasure and pride that growing one's own crops instils in each of us. Do not be misled by this foolish argument. There is no pleasure or pride to be found in growing crops; it is a misplaced form of masochism, brought on by some entirely independent guilt complex.

In all honesty, no one enjoys the back-breaking toil of turning a tough, unyielding sod. We pretend we do in order to justify the pain and discomfort we go through. Perhaps it helps alleviate the work ethic smouldering deep in our psyche. But that could be exercised just as easily and with far less expenditure of time and effort by simply visiting a good psychologist and undergoing therapy.

One further note of caution: the true test of any crop is that we accept it as we would one from a shop. How many times have you eaten a vegetable, only to be told by the proud owner that 'you couldn't tell it was home-grown, could you'? If this were the case, then surely we should cut out the tomfoolery. Why be deceived? We don't despise garages for selling us cars, or electrical shops for selling us kettles. Why then is such a stigma attached to the poor greengrocer?

Turnip Townsend

Turnip Townsend was the first of the great agricultural revolutionaries, taking his name from the quite remarkable achievements he made with turnips. Others were to follow: Parsnip Townsend who worked with parsnips, Cowslip Townsend who worked with cowslips, and the great Gymslip Townsend who worked with the local convent school and was never without a smile.

Among the great man's more illustrious descendants were:

TURNUP TOWNSEND Introduced the short trouser leg tied up with a piece of string and with a large baggy turn-up at the bottom, that is still popular today.

BURNUP TOWNSEND Introduced the young farmer in the Mark II Ford Escort who flies around narrow country lanes at ninety miles an hour.

BURNOFF TOWNSEND Introduced the practice of producing big black clouds of stubble smoke from farmland immediately adjacent to crowded motorway intersections on busy summer weekends.

TURNOFF TOWNSEND Introduced the overladen farm trailer with no indicator lights that starts to turn right the moment you pull out to overtake it.

Turnip Townsend.

SPINOFF TOWNSEND Female author who produces tee-shirts and records based on her bestselling book about a teenage boy.

OFFSPIN TOWNSEND Famous cricketer – nothing to do with gardening.

OFFSEASON TOWNSEND Winter holiday brochure produced by the Townsend-Thorenson organisation.

OFFSEASON GRAVESEND Type of holiday taken by those unable to afford the kind advertised in the OFFSEASON TOWNSEND brochure.

SEAOFF GRAVESEND What those on OFFSEASON GRAVESEND holidays spend most of their time watching (nothing to do with gardening either).

New ideas for improvement

Just as Townsend did in the past, the time is now ripe for modern growers to develop new and inspired innovations. We have already seen East Anglia turned into one colossal field and the hope must be that, in time, much of England will be reduced to one great treeless prairie as well.

But it is the crops we grow that offer the cultivator the greatest opportunities. What better example for us all to follow than that of the humble Kiwi, once a modest emigrant from New Zealand, but now the toast of restaurateurs? Already the Kiwi has arrived in England or, more correctly, in the Channel Islands where it has ousted tomatoes and salad crops from the greenhouses.

But this is only the tip of the iceberg, for the real breakthrough must surely be only round the corner with the arrival of the first ready-sliced Kiwi, a crop that avoids the unnecessary preparation of the fruit into tiny slivers and in fact produces tiny slices straight from the tree.

And this development doesn't only apply to the Kiwi. Why not plants that cater for other specific needs of the restaurant trade? The Mixed Fruit plant that offers a selection of apples, bananas, cherries, pineapples and strawberries straight off the one plant? A self-contained Fruit Cocktail tree which avoids the costly and messy business of actually collecting together and preparing all the ingredients that are required?

Talk of the pineapple leads us to the long-overdue need for the tinned pineapple plant: a plant that will give pineapple chunks and quarters just as we want them, freeing us from the tedious chores of washing, cutting and dicing.

What of innovation, I say? Where the Kiwi first trod, others must now be prepared to follow. Take the example of the prickly pear. Small, spiky and thoroughly indigestible it may appear on the outside, but what lies within? Even a tiny fleshy core of less than half a square inch is enough to warrant exploitation. Indeed, the less of the plant that is edible, the more desirable it appears to be. It acquires a scarcity value that would be totally lost if we could gobble up the whole fruit. Say we cut down a large prickly pear; we slice, trim, dress, skin, trim again, slice, crush . . . and what is left is five pounds of pure gold.

Why are there not great prickly pear plantations going up all over the countryside? Why are there not hundreds of acres of prize farmland being put under cacti? Inertia – that is why: reluctance among conservative farmers to dig up acres of unprofitable wheat and replant them with lucrative cactus. If we don't change soon, we will be left behind and the E.E.C. will have moved in and will be paying Danish pig farmers *not* to feed their sows on them.

Look at the number of food revolutions we have missed out on. Where were the watermelon fields when watermelons took off in our greenhouses? Where are our maize fields to provide those endless corn-on-the-cobs (?corns-on-the-cob) that keep the restaurant business alive? And what of passion fruit? Where are all the passion fruit growers to turn the English heartland back into a money-spinning paradise? Let's remember these examples when the cactus growers ask for our support. Remember that there still is not a cactus mountain in Europe. And ask yourself why!

Why has no one hit upon the idea of growing salads and vegetables entirely for the kebab trade? Tiny slices of tomato and cucumber, dried-up flakes of tough lettuce, shrivelled-up chillis: why is no one in Britain growing these? The demand is there – go into any kebab house and you will see for yourself. Why is no one investing capital in miniature greenhouses to grow just such crops?

Nowhere can this indolence be seen better than in the yoghurt trade. Each year a new yoghurt takes off and sweeps the market. Never is that yoghurt based on a *British* flavour. What about beef yoghurt; why are we not promoting prime beef-flavoured yoghurt? Or sugarbeet yoghurt? We have acres of sugarbeet – why not a yoghurt based upon it? Simply because the public has not been encouraged to buy it.

And therein lies the rub. For this is the other great area we must learn to cultivate – the consumer's mind. Beyond all these great advances in the field, the one final advance must lie in the mind and attitude of the housewife. We have encouraged her to accept British crops, to appreciate that shrivelled and misshapen fruit and vegetables are good. Let her know that Welsh-grown coffee, despite having a taste like coal dust, is better for her. Convince her that Scottish pineapples lose no flavour for being the size and flavour of small ball-bearings. Turnip Townsend did it with the swede and his namesake, and there is no reason why it shouldn't be done again.

Herbs

Herbs are used for two purposes: (a) to add a flavour that isn't there but should have been; and (b) to take away a flavour that is there that shouldn't be. There are only four common kinds of herb: mint, parsley, sage and thyme. Fennel, tarragon, sweet marjoram and savory are still used, though few (if any) people know why.

MINT Close to peppermint and spearmint. Not quite as close to Royal Mint and Dickie Mint (see Diddy Men of Knotty Ash not q.v.). Mint is cut and mixed with vinegar and sugar and used to garnish meat dishes. It smells 'minty', tastes 'minty', and apart from that there's not a lot else you can say about it.

PARSLEY Virtually tasteless. It is therefore added to virtually everything for virtually no reason at all. The word for this is 'garnish' which is a polite way of saying 'useless'. Garnish is an anagram that spells the word 'shinrag'. This doesn't mean anything but seems like a rather good word if you want another meaning for 'useless'.

SAGE Small hardy shrub which is used in stuffings. Sage also means someone wise or well informed. There is little that's wise about shoving tasteless leafy weeds up a chicken's bum – therefore the word sage probably derives instead from the word StrAnGE, which seems to describe the practice much better.

THYME Even less is known about this herb than about all the other herbs put together. It tastes of 'thyme' and is used when a dish requires a 'thyme' sort of flavour.

BASIL Not important as a herb but popular on account of its name. Diners finding a basil leaf in their meal often call out, 'Oh look, I've found a basil leaf'; whereupon all the other diners invariably perform impromptu pieces from 'Fawlty Towers'.

Fruit and vegetables

Fruit and vegetables are – as far as the gardener is concerned – exactly the same thing; one normally grows above the surface, and the other below it . . . But not always. And vice versa. And also versa vice. Apart from that one basic difference which, as it turns out, isn't a difference anyway, the two things are the same. Thus when you address a friend or colleague with the phrase 'hello, my old fruit', you could quite naturally replace it with the alternative 'hello, my old vegetable'. It is unlikely that this will do you much good, but you are entitled to do as you wish, and this must be the basis for any libel settlement you make out of court later.

> **OLD JOKE**
> Q: Is a date a fruit or a vegetable?
> A: I'll tell you in the morning.

Another difference between fruit and vegetables is that vegetables tend to be the more ugly of the two. Which after all is quite natural since they spend by far the greater part of their time hiding underground. Apart from that, there are absolutely no distinguishing features between the two. In fact there is very little else to be said about either that is of any real interest.

More appealing than the fruit and vegetables themselves is the number of techniques now employed to keep predators at bay when the crop is ripening in the field or garden.

Birds are generally seen as the greatest threat; and a great deal of energy is naturally expended in their general direction. A simple scarecrow or a line of tinkling tinfoil may prove useful. However, far more interesting (from a purely sensational point of view) is the range of field guns that fire random pellets at the birds after they have settled. (NOTE: Be careful not to enter any field or garden yourself without protection; a stout dustbin lid usually does the trick. Or you could try an armoured car; it's cheap to buy and virtually foolproof.) Remember that by far the greater part of any crop taken from a field where such a contraption is working is likely to be riddled with buckshot, so if you actually attempt to eat any you will run a very real risk of lead poisoning. However, that is not the point. What matters is that your vegetables and fruit have been saved and not lost to some thieving, grasping bird.

More interesting still than the use of strategic armaments is the newly developed anti-bird land-mine. Disguised as an ordinary swede or potato, this device contains over twelve pounds of high explosive (enough to blow a crater twenty-five feet deep) and certainly powerful enough to give any bird that tries to nibble it a very real fright. The mine also has the advantage of obviating the need for orthodox cultivation. Such a method of pest control is not, however, recommended for small gardens or those on roofs or terraces, nor is it recommended for window-boxes, where any form of explosive charge should in general be avoided.

Also of interest are the number of anti-rodent protections now on offer (that is to say, protections against rodents – not protectives with which rodents might arm themselves against attack; see completely different book on protective clothing and headgear for common rodents). Poison and traps are always popular, of course; but there is a good deal more fun to be had from taking a twelve-bore shotgun to some poor defenceless furry mite standing four feet away and blasting the pants off its backside with a couple of well-placed cartridges.

CAUTION: Do be careful when using a shotgun in a domestic situation. Ricochets are notoriously dangerous in this environment, as is mistaken identity, too. It comes as no real comfort to the bereaved owner of next door's hamster to learn that you hadn't established the poor creature's identity till after you had fired and reloaded three times.

Do remember too that shotguns should not be used to dispose of human pests. Pilferage of prize fruit and vegetables can be extremely annoying and upsetting, but it still isn't acceptable in the eyes of British justice to shoot a man for trying to pinch your marrow, unless of course you are very rich and dine regularly with the Chief Constable.

An interesting new approach to pest control is to be found in the development of the heat-seeking anti-rodent missile. Programmed correctly, the four-foot-long missile can seek out and destroy any small warm-blooded animal (such as a shrew or small fieldmouse) at a distance of some five hundred miles. The missile, a spin-off from the U.S. defence programme, can be launched either from land or from a submarine, all of which is very exciting but none too practical for the average gardener.

Magic mushrooms

This is the name given to any produce picked wild in a field, which has the appearance of a mushroom and which, when consumed, has the effect of making you feel funny.

The stigma attached to magic mushrooms is still a deterrent to many people. While there is something distinctly chic about drugs taken after dinner in an expensive Knightsbridge flat, there is definitely nothing chic about eating funny mushrooms, and, despite the similarity of their effect, the conspicuous difference in style is likely always to relegate the mushroom to the preserve of the left-over hippie.

Half the appeal of drugs must surely lie in the thrill of the unknown – and probably what prevents the magic mushroom from being accepted in fashionable society is its positive association with converted ambulances, wet wellingtons, smocks and free open-air concerts – an anachronistic link with a culture that is no longer with us, except in Welsh hill villages and a few very provincial universities.

It also lacks media appeal. You can hardly visualise the Drug Squad, complete with squad cars and air support, making a dawn swoop on a patch of bell mushrooms in a shady copse. Nor can you imagine a haul of a bagful of mushrooms by Heathrow customs officers making the front pages of the national press. What would have happened if the French Connection had hinged on a half-pound bag of button mushrooms being slipped through on a day trip to Boulogne? Perhaps it boils down, quite simply, to appearances. What more unprepossessing object could one imagine than a shrivelled and withered mushroom? Where is its style, its elegance, its glamour? Can you imagine a prison inmate confessing to his colleagues that he got four years for peddling this? Grass, yes – mushrooms, no.

Finally, a word on the mythology of the magic mushroom itself. Every year, a rumour spreads across the country that hundreds of battered and ageing Dormobiles are heading towards a secret rendezvous in Wales where another patch has been found. But has anyone ever seen this field? Or might it just be another of those strange stories that appear magically, rather like the mushrooms, on slow news days in summer?

Gardening manicures

EYESIGHT Place a slice of cucumber over one eye. Next, place a slice of cucumber over the other eye. Now remove both slices of cucumber. Notice how much better the eyesight is with the pieces of cucumber removed.

CARROTS Place a carrot in one ear and a carrot in the other ear. Now look in the mirror. Don't you look a real pratt!

TOMATOES Remember that a tomato pressed firmly into the cheeks during a meal is the ideal way to ruin the meal for anyone else present.

SKIN Skin that is hard and dry may be rubbed all over with half a banana lightly rubbed in salad cream. It won't actually do any good, but if that sort of thing turns you on . . .

CARROT Use a carrot to gently massage tired or swollen joints. Rub the carrot against the joint for several minutes. Be sure to remove any clothing before rubbing. Be careful to use discretion when preparing to use a carrot in this way. It is perfectly reasonable to rub a carrot against yourself without asking permission; however, you may cause alarm and despondency among more sensitive people if you suggest they remove their clothing simply to enable you to rub a carrot

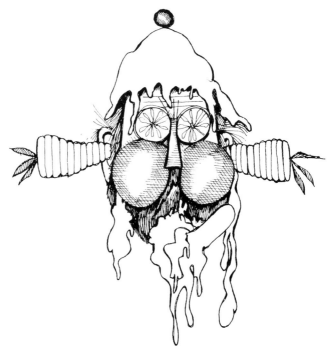

against them. It is as well to assure yourself that the person approached does in fact suffer from poor joints. Offering to rub a carrot against any part of a complete stranger who has not complained of any discomfort may be deemed unnecessarily forward.

LETTUCE LEAVES Lettuce leaves can improve the bust line if inserted carefully into the brassiere cups before wearing. Ensure that the leaves of the lettuce are clean and fresh, and free from grubs or insects. There can be few more distressing experiences than finding one's bosom heaving with the combined efforts of a dozen creepy-crawlies (then again, whatever turns you on . . .). Do ensure also that the lettuce leaves are not visible from outside the brassiere. Few ladies make a full recovery from the shock of having a male total stranger point out that a lettuce is frothing out of their cleavage. Should you be faced with this embarrassing situation, make light of the incident with a casual laugh and the unconcerned observation that this sort of thing happens all the time nowadays.

RASPBERRIES Raspberries can be inserted down the socks with great ease. This will of course serve no useful purpose and will merely make the feet extremely unpleasant and sticky; but it can be done if you feel like it, and there is nothing anyone can do to stop you. Even today, in peace-torn Britain. Do not insert raspberries down other people's socks without first obtaining their written consent. In some instances, the act of rolling down a stranger's socks and pressing soft fruit around their ankles has been construed by the courts to be a criminal offence.

SKIN CARE Face wrinkles can be easily removed by stroking a large turnip across the face for several hours each morning. By the time this exercise is over, the face will feel toned and refreshed. The rest of you will feel totally shattered – but at least your face will feel good.

LEMONS You can also balance a slice of lemon above each cheekbone, a pineapple cube over the nose, and a peach segment on the chin. This will do little to the face, but at least you'll (a) have something to eat if you become peckish and (b) be a wow at Hallowe'en.

SWEDES Do not rub the body with Swedes. If you do, they are liable to become overexcited and difficult to stop or restrain. If you *must* rub your body with Swedes, make sure there is a bucket of cold water present (see TWIGS and FLAGELLATION).

DANES On no account rub yourself all over with Danes.

GREAT DANES Rub yourself all over with Great Danes only under proper medical supervision.

GOOSEBERRIES Do not rub your body with gooseberries. If you do, they are likely to feel even more of a gooseberry than before.

5 THE GARDENER AS ARTIST

The colour and texture of plants are often as much a part of the garden as the life of the plants that grow there. Never mind that all are living in an environment unsuited to their welfare. Never mind that in a few weeks all will be dead. For now, just relish the colour and tone of the garden which is as much an artistic expression as it is one born of earth and soil.

The need to create a colourful, perfectly balanced backcloth has brought forth the artist/gardener for whom a landscape is a

canvas on which to spread his paint. His trowel and his fork are brush and palette-knife for the canvas on which he works. He is a painter. Not a cultivator.

Well, that's the theory. Read now the account of the gardener as artist by Cecilia Padgemore-Jones:

> I need to have a garden that expresses me. My love and my needs. That's why I love flowers. I love the way they move and say, 'Look at me, I'm a flower.'
>
> The most important thing to me about flowers is the colour. That's why, when I'm preparing a garden, I always think very carefully about colour. In particular I try to express my own colour through the colour of my flowers. This plant is green. This plant is not. I think that statements like that tell you a lot about the person whose garden it is. I find myself loving some of my plants more than people. Especially the ones that say, 'I am a plant, look at my colour.' I think it is very important for plants to make a statement about their colour. Colour is so important.
>
> Without colour I think plants would not be able to make statements and I like the way that the colour of a plant helps to delineate a gardener's own emotion. And I think that's very important. That's why when I buy a plant I feel I am buying a part of me. I feel that I am exposing myself and saying, 'Here I am. You are a plant. I am a woman.' I think this is very important.

Taken from *My Garden and Me* by Cecilia Padgemore-Jones, published by Coffee-Table Press, price £19.95 or (through all good remainder bookshops) £1.95.

Landscape design

The art of landscape design began in England in the eighteenth century. Previously, both in England and abroad, the immediate surrounds of a house consisted of a garden of walks, hedges, flowerbeds and people. In very formal gardens, a servant was often employed simply to direct the people using the garden and to ensure that house guests promenading the walks maintained a regular and pleasing pattern at all times.

During the eighteenth century, however, landowners began to take an interest in the land beyond their garden walls. Landscape design developed into an art form in its own right, thanks to men like William Kent, William Chambers and Culpability Brown. Enormous faith was placed in these great designers, since many of their projects did not reach fruition until long after those who had commissioned them had died.

Thus it was possible for many a cowboy designer to practise undetected, the follies of their ways not becoming evident until they had long since fallen off the twig (see TWIGS etc.). The most notable of these was without doubt Culpability Brown, who started work before the rest and was blamed for many of the great country house disasters of the period, notably: (a) BLENHILL HOUSE in Leicestershire, in which the magnificent gardens in front of the house opened upon a

perfect vista of a local rat-catcher's croft. (b) HILLHEAD PALACE in Scotland, where insufficient attention to the contouring of an artificial lake led to the house looking down on to a stretch of open water shaped like a pair of human buttocks. And (c) MARCHMORE GROVE in Kent, in which Culpability used all his lack of skill and judgement to lay out a garden in which, when it finally came to full flower some 100 years later, a twisting stream spelt out the phrase: 'Hi, Mum!' in perfect gothic script.

Culpability was of course not the only one guilty of or responsible for such palpable blunders.

STOKEY CARRUTHERS This worthy laid out an entire estate in North Norfolk using hired railway labour. The result was a landscape impressive for its sturdy construction and remarkably precise engineering, and less for its artistic merit – one half of the site being traversed by a series of embankments and cuttings, and the other by an arboreal version of a marshalling yard.

MAD HATCH BUCKLEY He actually pioneered a country estate for the Duke of Bogweed in which the lake rested on top of a high mound and, even after mild rain, water would cascade down its flanks, drenching not only the parkland but much of the house as well.

SIR KEMBLE JONES The baronet worked on several estates in the North of England. The most noteworthy feature of his work was his unattractive use of brick and iron to hold his parkland in place. Sir Kemble, a born worrier, was constantly afraid that his garden would collapse and insured against this by adding further buttresses that in the foulness of time gave the feature the prophetic air of future Urban Blight.

DUKE SIMON DE BUNGFORT The noble lord laid out his own magnificent estate at Marlborough; but he insisted that the local sandy loams were too poor for the exotic plants he intended to grow, and therefore added so much sea mud that, on the fateful day the owner inspected his handiwork, a brisk shower reduced the whole thing to a steaming facsimile of a giant cow-pat.

EDMUND HARKNELL An explorer and flamboyant architect, he attempted to introduce a tropical rainforest into his garden. He succeeded, and within weeks was eaten by a tiger (just outside Redditch).

Garden tips

The Garden Beautiful movement has provided much useful advice on how to rid yourself of garden tips. Unfortunately, the more effort one puts into concealing the unmentionables in one's garden, the more they seem to stand out. Hide a compost tip at the bottom of the garden and the eye will immediately travel towards it as though hypnotised. The correct technique is therefore to encourage a positive profile towards understanding unsightly objects. Learn to encourage in yourself as well as in others an appreciation of the ugly or unseemly, like these two women admiring discarded black plastic rubbish sacks in one of their gardens. It is an example that can be profitably followed with other rubbish as well.

1st Woman: What a wonderful arrangement!
2nd Woman: Do you like it?
1st: It's so *you.*
2nd: We wanted to create an arrangement that said:
     'This is me, these are my sacks.'
1st: How long did it take?
2nd: Well, we spent a long time discussing what we were
     going to do.
1st: It's so *totally* you. A statement.
2nd: Exactly, it's like we're saying – rubbish bags are . . .
1st: Are completely . . .!
2nd: Exactly!!

1st: What's underneath them?

2nd: The rest of the garden.

1st: Oh God, that's utterly brilliant!

2nd: D'you really think so?

1st: When I saw it I said, 'Tabitha, those sacks are you.'

2nd: We wanted to make a statement. A statement that said, 'Look at us, we're rubbish sacks.'

1st: What's in them?

2nd: Rubbish.

1st: That's brilliant.

2nd: D'you think so?

1st: Rubbish in rubbish sacks. It's so utterly perfect.

2nd: We wanted to apply for an Arts Council grant, but Marc said that would be too trad.

1st: Oh I agree – everyone is applying for Arts Council grants for their rubbish sacks these days.

2nd: I know, we wanted to create something that said, 'Look at me, I'm not an Arts Council Project.'

1st: It says so much about you both.

2nd: And yet it doesn't.

1st: Exactly. It says everything. And yet . . .

2nd: It says nothing.

1st: Brilliant.

2nd: We wanted a collection of rubbish bags that as soon as people saw it they would say, 'Oh God that's so ambiguous!'

1st: Oh God that's so ambiguous!

2nd: D'you think so?

1st: It's so ambiguous it's . . . it's not ambiguous.

2nd: D'you know, I believe you can really say something with rubbish sacks.

The garden in colour

Colour the garden to see how a garden changes colour through the seasons!

WINTER

1	White	6	White	11	White	16	White
2	White	7	White	12	White	17	White
3	White	8	White	13	White	18	White
4	White	9	White	14	White	19	White
5	White	10	White	15	White	20	White

SPRING (SORRY, BLACK AND WHITE ONLY AVAILABLE)

1	Grey	11	White (or Black) (or Grey)
2	Grey	12	White and Black
3	Black (or Grey)	13	Black and White
4	Grey (or Black)	14	Grey and Grey
5	Light Black	15	Off-grey
6	Dark White	16	Earl Grey
7	Off-black	17	Eddie Gray
8	Grey (or Grey)	18	May Gray
9	Grey	19	Grey
10	Grey	20	(see 1–19 inclusive)

AUTUMN

As above, but delete green and insert brown.

SUMMER

1	Green
2–20	(see above)

The gardener's colour chart

Use to identify every possible colour that can ever be found in the garden

Green	Brown	Brown & Green	Black
grass	soil	some plants	slugs

Green	Brown	Brown & Green	Black
plants	more soil		moles

Green	Brown	muddy lawnmowers	Black
weeds	more soil		flies

Green	Brown	Brown & Green	Black
lawnmower	dead plants	very ill animals	fingernails

Green			Black
hosepipe	Brown	Brown & Green	extremely muddy lawnmowers
	dead weeds	some armed tanks	

Green			
leaves	Brown		Black

Green	dead leaves	Brown & Green	clouds
fingers		some aircraft	Blue

	Brown		language
	animals		

6 THE GARDENER'S ALMANAC

The gardener's almanac is a hardy annual that appears once a year on publishers' book lists, and provides a rich crop of good healthy bestsellers for many.

Generally grown on bookshop shelves just before Christmas, the almanac can often be left for years without the leaves once opening.

Definition of gardening phrases

Annual Any plant which, were it to have lived, would have flowered only once a year.

Avocado Fruit which may be grown by piercing with a needle and balancing over the top of an old jam jar till hairs grow through. (It is not known how avocados manage to find the necessary jam jars when grown in the wild.)

Bed That in which a gardener spends his happiest hours.

Biennial Any plant which, were it to have lived, would still have died, albeit more slowly.

Brochure Form of light fiction by which a gardener can assess what his garden would have looked like, had it not been his garden.

Bugs That which constantly annoys.

Cactus That plant which requires minimal attention and in return attracts ditto.

Christmas tree Evergreen tree that is ever losing its needles. The average Christmas tree grows three feet longer between the time of purchase and the time of erection in the living-room, some twenty minutes later.

Dog A form of automatic digger suitable for turning over any garden.

Dormant A plant that isn't.

Fence An imaginary line that once identified the division between two former gardens.

Fig That which is not given at regular intervals.

Forcing 1) The act of encouraging a plant to perform an unnatural act and flower. 2) The act of placing a too-small plastic bag over the tops of delicate plants by garden centre assistants.

Fruit Seed of plant that does not appear when you want it to, but which appears in great profusion the moment you go away on holiday.

Furrow Straight line occurring across a gardener's forehead.

Gin Famous agricultural aid developed by distillers.

Grape Fruit which can be picked and trodden to produce red feet (and/or socks).

Ground nut One who is expert on matters of the earth. A Friend of the Earth.

Harrowing Gardener's experience that produces furrow (q.v.).

Hedge Shrubbery that imagination can turn into a straight line.

Hoe Gardening tool used to remove toenails somewhere between the first and second joints.

Honesty Attractive plant used to conceal unattractive crack or subsidence during a house sale (dishonesty).

Hose Rubber tube used to water six separate parts of the garden at the same time. Also used to remove attractive plants that have not been removed by mismanagement.

Insect Any creature that conflicts with the gardener's own interpretation of a balanced ecosystem.

Insecticide Spray used to destroy that part of the environment on which insects do not live.

Lawn A number of sods that becomes one large sod later in life.

Mulch Sound of wellington boot being removed from especially boggy piece of ground.

Parasite Anything which exists to take energy from a garden without providing a useful return. Examples include: electric clippers, electric mowers, children, pets, family.

Path That which, irrespective of cultivation, provides the shortest distance between two points in a public garden.

Pinching Latin-American form of pruning.

Prune An unsuccessful gardener.

Rock Garden 1) Garden in which hardier plants may be set advanced survival exercises. 2) Noisy Hamburgery in Soho.

Root Any part of a plant that remains under the surface until a foot comes near (see DOG).

Rot Inappropriate gardening advice.

Seed That which theoretically grows into a plant.

Soil Type of dark mud; in short supply in the garden but readily available on freshly cleaned kitchen floors.

Sprinkler Convenient device for watering other people's lawns, cars, clothes-lines, barbecues.

Stump What remains after any garden implement encounters one.

Toadstool Mushroom with homicidal tendencies.

Tool Anything which is used for purposes other than that for which it was intended.

Topiary The art of camouflaging a perfectly reasonable hedge to make it look like a deformed giraffe mating with a one-legged kangaroo.

Vegetable A tuber that, when grown with care and attention and carefully tended, tastes exactly like the frozen ones you buy in the shops.

Weed A plant described as being of unknown parentage by those referring to it.

Gardener's equipment

Axe Used for destroying any crop that cannot be destroyed by negligence.

Barrow Used to transport one unsightly spot to another unsightly spot.

Dibbler Used for dibbing (dibbing: the act of expending twice the effort to plant seeds which are not going to take root anyway).

Edging iron Used to improve the edge of a lawn. If used to excess, can lead to improvement of the edge of a lawn which no longer exists.

Grub Not a creature but an instrument used to remove weeds on lawn. Not to be used when weeds cover over 50% of the surface of the lawn or when lawn covers more than four square feet.

Hoe Used to turn over soil and hide weeds for a short while.

Lawnmowers Used to mow lawns, feet, wellington boots, etc.

Pails/Watering cans Used to water plants when appeals to divine sources have failed.

Rake Used to rake together clippings, leaves, rubbish, etc. Also used to produce a sudden, sharp sensation to unsuspecting forehead.

Riddle Used to sift soil (see also Watering (alternative)).

Spade Essential for turning over soil and digging holes. Small spades are called hoes. Large spades are called large spades.

Gardening in foreign lands

FRANCE The French are not gardeners; in France, interest in gardening rates somewhere between interest in test-match cricket and interest in plumbing ... and marginally less than interest in speaking English. The only gardens worth noting in France are the gardens (jardins) at Versailles, and le jardin (garden) de (of) Max Factor.

THE LOW COUNTRIES The Dutch produced the bulbs to produce the flowers to produce the inspiration behind the song 'Tulips from Amsterdam' by Max Bygraves. They have never been forgiven.

GERMANY The Germans don't like gardening, but they do like going into other people's gardens and claiming them for themselves. German interest in gardening rates somewhere between British interest in gardening and Icelandic interest in gardening.

ICELAND [deleted, due to lack of gardens]

THE MIDDLE EAST The only difference between Middle Eastern gardens and European gardens is that Middle Eastern gardens can be hoovered all over, and rolled up and taken with you when you move.

AUSTRALIA Gardening interest in Australia rates somewhere between interest in Australian cricket and interest in English cricket.

AMERICA In the past, the Americans have sent support to gardeners in South East Asia; now they are keen on supporting gardeners in Central and South America.

Types of garden

ROCK GARDEN Ideal garden for beginners. Rocks are easy to grow and require very little attention. In general, you should attempt to grow as many different rocks as possible, especially big rocks that cover a lot of space. As a general rule, a rock garden should contain 96–98% rocks.

ROSE GARDEN Rose gardens are like rock gardens. Except that they have fewer rocks and more roses. Many experts nowadays believe a rose garden should have very few rocks indeed, and certainly not nearly as many as a rock garden. However, there is a strong belief among many gardeners that rose gardens should be exactly like rock gardens, with the rose plants cut down and covered by rocks.

Remember, roses can be very prickly to touch. So do try and ask their permission first.

HERB GARDEN Herb gardens contain few rocks and few roses, but an extremely large number of herbs. Not as prickly as a rose garden but with fewer stones than a rock garden. (For the technically minded, it is common for a herb garden to contain no rocks or roses but a large number of herbs. Where herbs are not available, use rocks.)

WATER GARDEN Contains no herbs or roses. Contains rocks; but these are difficult to spot, as they sink the moment they are planted. Generally contains waterlilies and also carp, as opposed to ordinary gardens; the latter contain no carp at all as they are very difficult to plant, wriggle out of the hand and jump away the moment they're put in the soil.

KITCHEN GARDEN Contains no herbs, rocks, roses or water. Does not even contain a kitchen – which makes the whole thing very confusing and awkward. Kitchen gardens generally grow all the things that are required in the kitchen. Except, of course, kitchen equipment. The only place where kitchen equipment is grown in the garden is in the happy farm.

ROOF GARDEN A garden on a roof. Roof gardens are usually grown on flat, not sloping, roofs where there is less likelihood of them slipping down the side and falling off.

HANGING GARDEN A roof garden in the process of falling off.

Types of soil

CLAY Thick, heavy soil with predisposition to absorb water. Difficult to turn when wet. Difficult to turn when dry. Difficult to remove from boots, shoes and all forms of footwear (usually requires a carpet to remove thickest clay). Clay surfaces are usually best treated by planting with (a) paving slabs, (b) paving slabs, (c) paving slabs or (d) nothing.

SAND Thin, friable soil. Easy to dig and easy to turn. Unfortunately, not much use for plants so there is little point in bothering with it. Can be mixed with clay to produce a heavy, thick soil that is still not much use to plants.

LOAMS Any soil that is neither clay nor sand. The exact nature and composition of a loam is largely unknown, so the title can therefore be readily applied to almost any soil of uncertain origin. Sandy loams are often called sandy loams (to distinguish them from loams that aren't all that sandy).

LIGHT SOILS Soils which are light in weight on the spade are called 'light'. This does not mean they are so light they will simply rise up off the ground and float away. It does, however, mean they are so light that you may be faced with a difficult task when looking for a suitable reason not to dig them over.

HEAVY SOILS Heavy soils are characterised by peat. In between light soils and heavy soils are light-heavyweight soils and welterweight soils.

OTHER SUITABLE NAMES FOR SOILS (for use by gardeners when the subject turns to soil):

On the turn	Beamish	Bodey
Tricky	Surrey	Doyle
Ticklish	Light Middle	Shilton
Green	Lymington Toady	Beadle
Boamish	Old Thatcher	Wilmslow
Sponky	Boddington	Partridge
Marthe	Starg	New Malden

Saints of the garden

St Rita: Patron saint of the collapsible sun-lounger
St Trev: Patron saint of rustic garden furniture

St Elvis: Patron saint of the hose-reel connection that bursts loose just as you lean out to tighten it up

St Gary: Patron saint of the phallic-looking cactus your aunt gave you at Christmas without realising why everyone was laughing

St Nobby: Patron saint of the hover mower that goes over a lump of dog's droppings just as you bend down to find out why the blade isn't cutting as well as it should be

St Sheila: Patron saint of the three dead goldfish floating on the surface of the fishpond

St Tracy: Patron saint of gnomes

St Hippy: Patron saint of the weed

St Neville: Patron saint of the allotment

St Dotty: Patron saint of the swede, the carrot and the turnip; and of some models of early electric hedge-clippers *c.* 1968–75

St Jimmy: Patron saint of the leak

Potting

THE POTTER'S WORLD

POTTING The act of putting into pots

PUTTING That which occurs during most acts of potting

PITTING That which occurs when a pot is put on pitted ground (irrelevant)

PETTING See chapter of sexual foreplay (not included in this book)

PATTING See PETTING (above)

RE-POTTING The act of putting into pots for a second time

RE-PUTTING That putting which occurs after a previous act of putting

RE-PITTING That which occurs when a pitted pot is pitted for a second time (extremely irrelevant)

RE-PETTING See separate chapter on sexual problems (not included in this book)

RE-PATTING Often associated with RE-PETTING (q.v.)

POTTING ON Term of cordial friendship among gardeners
PUTTING ON Term of cordial friendship among putters
PETTING ON Term of cordial friendship among petters
RE-POTTING ON See RE-PUTTING ON
RE-PUTTING ON See RE-PITTING ON
RE-PITTING ON See RE-PETTING ON
RE-PETTING ON See RE-PATTING ON
RE-PATTING ON See RE-POTTING ON

How to cope with garden centres

Most garden centres are designed along purely military lines;
their aim is to instil confusion, panic, demoralisation, and
ultimately total and unconditional surrender. To survive the
garden centre, a useful tactic is to make a swift early purchase
of a large and bulky plant. This immediately renders the arms
inoperative and therefore reduces the ability to make any
further purchases.

Remember that garden centres are there to make money . . .
not to serve the needs of the gardener. Consider what you are
paying for before you buy: you are paying for the privilege of
getting another man to do a job you yourself cannot be
bothered with. Any price you pay should take this fact into
account; it is not like a normal purchase, where you buy
something which you are incapable of providing yourself; in
garden centres, the bulk of the items *can* be produced by the
consumer. If it is worth your while getting another man to
waste his time raising plants for you, then you may indeed feel
that it is money well spent. If not, then consider long and hard
before you buy. Remember: garden centres offer little more
than surrogate parenthood for plants and the amount you
spend there should reflect the value you put on such a service.

THE LANGUAGE OF THE GARDEN CENTRE (taken
from the Dictionary of English–Garden Centre/Garden
Centre–English)

Assistant says	*Translation*
I'll get someone to help you	I'll get someone to help me
It will grow anywhere	It's a weed
It needs plenty of sunlight	It doesn't stand much chance outside of the tropics
You'll probably find it will die back a bit	Don't blame us if you get it home and find it's dead
Try and keep it in the shade	Try and keep it where you can't see how bare it is
It doesn't need much food	It doesn't need much food because it's dead
Maybe you overwatered it	I'm not blaming anybody, but it's your fault
Maybe you didn't water it enough	I'm not blaming you, but there are only two people in this room whose fault it could have been, and it's not me
Perhaps the soil was too rich/poor	It's still your fault
It's meant to look like that	It's meant to have bright blue spots all over it
It's the ideal present	It's cheap
That's just the sap coming out	It's a triffid
They hibernate like that	It's July
It's a common lobelia	It was a common lobelia
It's a dwarf rose	It's a full-size rose that hasn't grown

Paths and pathways

Well-planned paths are useful for walking about your well-unplanned garden. Remember: paths need less watering or attention than plants and are therefore an extremely valuable addition to your landscape. A path should be planned with care and with consideration. When you come to lay it, that planning should be ruthlessly forgotten and the path laid with utter abandon. But, at least at the planning stage, it is good to have firm ideas.

The surface material of the path may be asphalt, gravel, ashes, bricks, concrete, stone slabs (select any five from six). In addition, your path should contain cracks/puddles/weeds/moss/oil/motor vehicles/caravans. Asphalt is easy to lay (especially if you arrange for someone else to do it for you) and can provide an easy way of covering all loose and unwanted materials quickly and efficiently.

Do make sure pets are kept indoors during asphalt laying. There are few more annoying sights than discovering one's prize wolfhound fossilised beneath the surface of a new driveway and you will find yourself torn between the rival demands of saving your pet and saving your new all-weather surface.

Gravel is a more practical substitute. Loose and movable objects trapped beneath gravel present far fewer problems to the path layer. Gravel should be spread in a random pattern over a large area, so that path users can be left to decide for themselves where exactly the line of path may be. Fresh gravel should be added periodically to replace that trodden away; this should be done at infrequent intervals, not every time a visitor is suspected of making off with your precious gravel on his boots. There can be few more distasteful sights than that of a long-lost relative visiting the house for the first time in thirty years, only to be confronted at the front door by an irate householder asking him to account for the gravel that now lodges in the treads of his shoes.

Ashes may be used as a substitute for gravel. Do not lay ashes straight from the fire; a number of unfortunate incidents in which car tyres have been badly scorched and burnt by driving over fresh ashes have been recorded, and several cases of dinner guests leaving, only to find their cars resting on four charred and blackened pillars.

Bricks are often a better alternative. Bricks can be laid in many interesting patterns to create a path; unfortunately, this requires considerable time and effort and is not normally worth either expenditure. The easiest way to lay a brick path is to build a brick wall then, having allowed it to set solid, rest with one's back against it and, heaving firmly, push the whole thing over on to the ground. Leave the bricks as they fall; the ragged and uneven surface will convey an impression of great age. To complete the effect, empty the liquid contents of the shed and greenhouse over the bricks to add a broad selection of stains and splash marks.

Concrete, though not decorative, is cheap and long-lasting. At all costs AVOID MIXING CONCRETE YOURSELF. For large quantities, a cement-mixer lorry may be hired to deliver the concrete, ready mixed and on site. Alternatively, for small quantities try stopping a cement-mixer lorry in the street and offering a fiver for a few bucketfuls of the stuff to the driver. Most cement lorries can be manoeuvred across lawns, flowerbeds and fences to reach the desired location for the concrete. For crazy paving (see below), try and encourage the driver to reverse his lorry via the freshly laid path.

Stone/pre-cast slabs are suitable for most surfaces. To prepare for 'crazy paving', simply lay the flags down on a rough or unprepared surface and walk over them in thick, heavy boots. The slabs will crack and break easily to give you the desired result.

Pond care

Ponds are large puddles. Remember that and you will not go far wrong. Why people should wish to ornament their gardens with large puddles is still a mystery. But augment them they do ... and often with dire results.

The primary problem with ponds is their need for water. Were it to be possible to design a pond with no water, then one would undoubtedly be on to a winner. Alas, at the moment all ponds require a greater or lesser amount of water, sitting, flowing, dribbling, up, down, across or through them.

In addition, ponds tend to encourage weeds, fountains and fish. Fish die, fountains break down, and weeds grow. There is little else to add. Your pond will look better for neglect. Indeed, the more neglected you can persuade it to look, the more acceptable the results will turn out to be. Once you have achieved the appearance of a derelict bomb-crater, then you will have reached a satisfactory level.

Squirting

Squirting covers that vast range of sprays/powders/tablets/ solutions which can be used to keep at bay everything except what you actually want to keep at bay. Use elementary precautions when spraying: spray away from the wind; spray away from people you know or are friendly with; spray only outdoors. Powders require less care and should be applied liberally and without attention to instructions.

When using sprays, it is only fair to keep all pets indoors. However, since when did fairness come into germ warfare? A new and practical alternative to conventional spraying is currently available to owners of model aircraft who can now spray their plants and crops from the air, just like the professionals, using air-drop weed-killers. Gardeners wishing to economise on this technique should use paper aircraft, to the wings of which a sachet of poison is attached and which may then be thrown from an upper-storey window to pass over the infestation.

Rubbish

Rubbish is a common problem for many gardeners. Try to avoid rubbish from accumulating by simply not raising a finger in the garden. Remember: the less work you do, the less rubbish you will generate and the easier your job will become.

If you must generate rubbish, then it can be deposited in the ordinary dustbin without any problems. Do not dispose of cement or hardcore in this way, however. A rockery is a good solution – rubbish of this type can be used to assemble a quite impressive rock garden; but do warn your neighbours if the final structure is likely to stand more than fifteen feet high.

Hedges

Frankly, a non-starter. Use a concrete and wood construction for all fences. 'Hedges', being of 'plant' construction, are likely to grow and cause no end of problems. Remember that in Britain it is your neighbour's duty to replace all fences unless you are proved guilty.

7 THE GARDENER'S STATISTICAL SUPPLEMENT

Modern gardening is just as much a science as modern football or modern darts or modern angling. Indeed, so scientific is modern gardening that in years to come we may quite possibly be able to plan and cultivate gardens along purely mathematical grounds.

The age of the slide-rule analogue gardener has at last arrived; and with it we must say goodbye to old-fashioned and outmoded ways, and turn instead to the computer and the calculator to cultivate the soil.

We must learn how to measure both work and achievement quantitatively. No longer is the garden a matter for subjective conjecture. It is a place where the coolly rational analytical techniques of the laboratory should be observed.

To this end we should be prepared to swap our wellingtons and overalls for the program analyst's handbook. It is more logical. It is more precise. And above all – and if nothing else has convinced you, then this will – it avoids any need to go outside.

The gardener's book of records

The most boring gardening fact in the world
The most boring gardening fact in the world comes from China and concerns the size of the stem of a plant that was last seen in 1927 and is of no possible interest to anyone.

The most intelligent plant in Britain
The most intelligent plant in Britain is a foxglove called Harry, grown in the front garden of Mr and Mrs Titweed's house in

Bexleyheath. The plant is capable of very very primitive thought patterns and enjoys watching 'Blankety Blank'.

The most talkative plant in Britain
There is no record of a plant ever having said anything.

This is either because plants are very very rude and never speak, or plants are very very deaf and can't hear what anyone says to them. Perhaps, they *cannot* speak.

The least politically motivated plant in the world
The least politically motivated plant in the world is an iris in Fife, Scotland, that during the 1974 General Election voted for the Scottish Nationalist Party.

The least exciting shrubbery in England
The least exciting shrubbery in England is to be found in Gloucester and is so uninspiring that a special warning was erected to warn passers-by of its dullness.

The largest gnome in the world
The largest garden gnome in the world comes from Iceland and is called Erickson; it measures 2 feet 8 inches in height.

The smallest gnome in the world
The smallest comes from Japan. It is $1\frac{1}{2}$ inches high, and is dressed as a bonzai lumberjack.

The fastest reproducing plant in the world
The fastest bonking plant in the world is the Bonking (*Bonkamus Bonalotii*) of Siam. It reproduces itself every thirty-eight seconds, and in half an hour can reproduce more times than the average visitor on a Club 18–30 holiday.

The longest continuous period of lawnmowing
The longest period of continuous lawnmowing without a break took place on 14 March 1977 when Mr Derick Nobbins of Hartlepool succeeded in mowing his own 10 foot by 8 foot lawn continuously for a period of just over 487 hours. At the end of that time the lawn was some fifteen feet nearer sea level than when he started.

The most tangled hose
The most tangled garden hose (as opposed to the most tangled anatomical hose) occurred on 11 June 1965 when an amateur gardener from Diss in Norfolk succeeded in tangling up not only his own hose but fourteen others in the neighbourhood. The mess took thirty-one days and three marriages to untangle.

The heaviest pansy in Britain
Records are not kept for the heaviest pansy in Britain. A pansy that was cut in 1973 weighed 37 tons, but it had a lorryload of fresh soil still attached. This record still stands.

The most violent act of potting
The most violent act of potting took place on 4 March 1923 when eleven shire horses and a traction engine were employed

by an irate gardener in order to plant a number of cuttings in his garden greenhouse. The greenhouse remained firmly locked during the potting operation, the traction engine and horses simply trampling over it until the whole affair was flattened.

The deepest piece of weeding
Many examples of unique burrowing to plant a new shrub have been registered, but the most remarkable was that of Harry Evans, from Stockton near Darlington, who hit a disused mineworking and plunged three hundred feet below ground. He survived with only minor bruising. No record was kept as to the fate of the plant.

The least useful garden tool ever invented
The least useful garden tool ever invented was the Mark II Sponkleturner, that was developed to remove the corners of plastic gro-bags. It can also be used to measure the amount of condensation found inside a wellington while still in use. It cost £83.99 and was an immediate sell-out.

The most offensive-looking gro-bag
The last record of this competition taking place was in 1975 when the first-prize rosette was mistakenly slapped on a prominent lady councillor, the resulting furore convincing the organisers that they should abandon all future contests.

The most saucy incident involving a gardener
[deleted, due to lack of information]

The most crazy crazy-paving in the world
The most crazy crazy-paving in the world occurred around, and subsequently inside, the home of Mr Arnold Pocklethorpe, when a 17-ton earth mover ran amok across his paved forecourt and into the house.

The deepest garden pond in Britain
The deepest garden pond in Britain belongs to Ted and Iris

Grimface who together dug an eight by eight foot pond to a depth of ninety-six feet because 'it seemed like a good idea'. The pond was subsequently filled in after a council order had been served on the property.

The fewest number of years spent as a student without coming into contact with a rubber plant

Incidents of students coming into contact with rubber plants are so common that in 1978 the N.U.S. set up a monitoring service to register levels of exposure suffered by students. The lowest, by Open University students working at home and not coming into contact with other students, revealed a minimum incidence of one encounter per month. No level that gave an exposure rate of nil was registered.

The least successful attempt at cross-fertilising two plants

An attempt was made to cross-fertilise a cactus and a dandelion in 1952. The result, a dandecactus, was destroyed by the public health inspector. A cross-fertilisation between a creeping bent and a copper beech to produce a bent copper has never been confirmed.

The most successful attempt to remove weeds

Generally accredited to the U.S.A.F. during a prolonged period of weed control, carried out on the Vietnamese mainland. The technique, which involved large quantities of napalm, was not successful in Britain.

High explosive was tried in Great Britain between 1939 and 1945. This only led to National Car Parks.

The most erogenous part of a plant

Plants do not have erogenous zones. It would be very difficult and frustrating even if they did, for they propagate their species away from the plant and therefore would experience little pleasure during a sexual encounter. The least erogenous part of a plant is probably its dead leaves.

The fastest growing 'living rock' plant in the world
A living rock plant that has grown 0.0000000000000001 mm in 53 years in Kansas, U.S.A., is regarded as the world record-holder for this event.

The most exciting thing ever to involve a cactus
Cacti are not exciting. The most exciting thing that has ever occurred to a cactus is starring in a number of successful American Westerns, and appearing twice on 'The Price Is Right'.

The least helpful piece of advice offered by an assistant in a garden centre
'Can I help you . . .?'

The wittiest thing ever said by a tree surgeon
Tree surgeons are not witty by nature. The wittiest thing ever recorded as being said by a tree surgeon is: 'This tree will have to come down'; this was not immediately hailed as witty until the tree was felled and discovered to be a telegraph pole.

The greatest number of gardeners killed by a single wheelbarrow
Seven (Poland).

The least number of wheels on a wheelbarrow
None.

The fastest watering of a garden
About 0.3 seconds, by the Royal Air Force on the occasion of the Dambusters raid on Northern Germany in which several hundred acres of gardens were watered in seconds, thanks to the Bouncing Bomb.

The ugliest potato ever grown in Britain
The evil potato of Montrose has long been considered the most wickedly evil potato ever to have been dug from the soil.

The biggest compost heap ever made in Britain

The biggest compost heap ever made was constructed in England during the early 1970s; it later became known as Telford.

The biggest compost heap in the world

(See Telford.)

The most expensive garden tool ever invented

The Bogglestick trimmer. Made out of gold, encrusted with diamonds and finished with an emerald hanging hook, the trimmer retails at some £96,000. Only one was ever made. It was left outside on the first night, and it rusted.

The greatest incline by a greenhouse

The greatest angle of incline on a greenhouse is accurately measured as 86° off true for a greenhouse in Northern England during the summer of 1959. The greenhouse, which was still used at this point, collapsed soon after when a dead leaf fell on it.

The greatest number of gardening books on a single bookshelf

The honour for the greatest number of books on a single shelf goes to Bogdust and Trotman. In 1983 this firm of booksellers achieved the remarkable total of 798 different gardening books on one shelf. Of these, three were eventually sold (one returned unread), and a further two stolen (both returned unread).

The largest pumpkin in Britain

The largest pumpkin in Britain was measured as being 96 inches in girth and weighing 974 lb. This was a remarkable achievement for a plant which has absolutely no practical value and which, after a string of personal appearances and displays up and down the country, was eventually hacked up and disposed of on the local rubbish tip at dead of night when no one was watching.

The longest period between emptying the grass-box of a lawnmower

Undoubtedly the record must go to Benny Buggerfist who kept the same grass-box attached and unemptied for a period of forty-seven years. During this time the grass in the box decomposed to soil and produced a near-perfect display of crocuses which did much to enhance the beauty of the machine. When the box was at last removed for cleaning, the machine completely broke down and could never be made to work again.

The greatest number of gardeners in one wellington

Regular competitions to insert the greatest possible number of gardeners into one wellie are commonplace – and, in several English counties, compulsory. Several notable instances of multiple occupation of one wellie by gardeners not even realising what they were doing have been noted, but in competition the record stands at eight (seven men and one woman) at Blockhampton in 1947. Eventually the wellington had to be removed surgically.

The first nudist rose grower

Almost certainly appeared on 11 March 1961.

The last nudist rose grower

Almost certainly appeared on 11 March 1961.

The first man to grow roses by hypnosis

The Great Alfonso claimed to have perfected the first hypnotic horticultural act during the 1953 summer season at Rhyl. However, a scandal broke out amongst the Rose Growers' Association; under the threat of physical violence, Alfonso removed this part of his performance from his repertoire.

The greenest fingers in the world

Belonged to 'King' Rhubarbs, a legendary eighteenth-century gardener much employed by the aristocracy, who, it was claimed, had fingers that glowed the colour of 'Sire Green' at night. King Rhubarbs was often used at firework exhibitions as a support act; in later years he travelled the kingdom performing with his 'illuminated fingers', gardening having to take a secondary role. His fingers were removed at death and are rumoured to haunt Ardley Heath on full-moon nights.

The most interesting thing ever said about a Kiwi fruit
Without exception, Kiwi fruits have totally failed to elicit any form of interesting comment. Probably the most interesting thing said has been: 'These Kiwi fruits are quite nice, aren't they?' which is marginally more interesting than 'They come from New Zealand, don't they?'.

The world record for concreting over a garden
The fastest piece of garden concreting took place on the southern Italian island of Sicily where the local 'Mafia' garden centre successfully concreted a garden, house, car and family of four, in 4 minutes 38 seconds.

The funniest story involving a Venus fly-trap
The funniest story ever to involve a Venus fly-trap concerns the one kept by a Mr Leonard Stubbley of Carshalton. He once inspected the bloom of his fly-trap by leaning forward inside the plant's open head. No sooner had he done so than the leaves closed around him, trapping him in a vicious headlock. Unable to remove the trap, he saw that his only chance of escape from the plant's clutches lay in attracting the attention of a passer-by. He stood at the picture window of his house for several hours, plant and flowerpot stuck to his head, waving frantically. When no one paid the slightest attention, eventually he despaired and rushed out into the street to try and get a passing motorist to take him to the local hospital. With the plant stuck firmly to his head, his visibility was of course minimal; running out into the road without warning, he immediately went beneath the wheels of a passing juggernaut. Luckily, he escaped with slight bruising; the plant (which the shock of the accident had removed from his head) suffered only light leaf-mould. The juggernaut unfortunately was a write-off.

The least practical use for a cactus
Jeremy Twittery of Glamorgan has a cactus that he uses instead of toilet tissue.

The most violent act with a tulip
Hardnose Higgins, the Wild Tulip Man of 'B' Wing, once attacked another man on his corridor with a tulip. The famous 'tulip' gang that Higgins formed after leaving prison used to control much of London's East End with a mixture of violence, intimidation and tulips. The gang was broken up by the police, but many of the tulips were never caught.

The shortest hosepipe in Britain
This measured three inches from tap to spout (Manchester, 1938). A one-inch hose, sold throughout Scotland in 1967, was also widely successful.

The most powerful hover mower in Britain
Developed and launched on 4 March 1975, this was capable of hovering some eighteen feet above the ground. Totally impractical in terms of cutting grass, if you stood under it for long enough it gave a very nice blow-wave.

The most successful roof garden kept by a lighthouse keeper
The obvious and predictable lack of space around most modern lighthouses has led to the use of the lighthouse roof as a suitable location for plants. The most – and, in turn, the least – successful garden was the hanging garden of Edison that hung down from the roof of the structure, completely obscuring the light itself.

The least contented owner of a new lawn
It is generally agreed that this was Talbot Grove of Redditch. He was on his hands and knees inspecting the soil surface when 'Rapido-Lawns' arrived and in seconds had laid an entire surface that covered not only the soil but also Mr Grove as he knelt there. The problem was cruelly exacerbated when

the workers noticed Mr Grove crawling about under the lawn, trying to get out; assuming he was an extremely large mole, they attempted to club him to death.

The most unusual use for a garden roller
The most unusual use for a garden roller was an attempt to put an end to a particularly hardy and well-rooted vine. Despite the unprovoked attack by the roller, the vine survived. The roller had to be scrapped.

The greatest number of marriages destroyed by a weed
The record number of marriages destroyed by a single weed is estimated to be fifteen. This occurred in Tunbridge Wells in 1978 when the effect of a solitary weed was to break up six marriages directly; a further nine were dissolved as partners sought to re-marry elsewhere. In California, lawyers acting for 87 petitioners cited one weed as co-respondent in all cases.

The most dribbly watering can in Britain
This was owned by a Mr Rupert Holmes of Dagenham. The watering can was reputedly so leaky that, even when it was entirely empty, it would continue to dribble heavily for a further thirty minutes.

The most interesting thing ever done by a fish in a fishpond
[deleted, due to lack of interest]

Relaxometer –
the cultivator's calculator . . .

The cultivator's calculator estimates the number of calories burned up in a range of various activities in the garden. It provides a quick and easy means of measuring the work involved in any task at hand. For example:

Digging up a weed burns up	10 calories
Planting a weed burns up	2 calories

(It is therefore far better to plant weeds than to dig them up.)

Lighting a pipe (large)	20 calories
Lighting a pipe (small)	10 calories
Lighting a pipe (hose)	[not applicable]
Looking at something	2 calories
Looking at something in a skirt	5–100 calories

Digging for five minutes	200 calories
Watching someone digging for five minutes	10 calories
Mowing a medium-sized lawn	150 calories
Not mowing a small-size lawn	0 calories
Not mowing a large-size lawn	0 calories
Mowing an artificial lawn	$\frac{1}{2}$ calorie

Putting on wellington boot (loose)	15 calories
Putting on wellington boot (tight)	560 calories
Sitting down doing nothing all day	$\frac{1}{2}$ calorie per hour
Watering garden with watering can	80 calories
Watering garden with hose	30 calories
Watering garden with rainwater	0 calories
Feeding fish	12 calories
Feeding dead fish	0 calories
Picking fresh fruit	200 calories per hour
Picking fresh fruit from shelf at Tesco	5 calories
Watching somebody else picking fruit from shelf	1 calorie
Brushing up leaves	30 calories
Not brushing up leaves	0 calories
Not brushing up some more leaves	0 calories
Not brushing up even more leaves	0 calories

8 TECHNICAL NOTES

Electrical gardening

There are any number of energy-saving gadgets now available to the gardener: electrical hedge-clippers, lawnmowers, weeders, cultivators, propagators. All aid the gardener in his battle against nature. But if technology takes its toll here as elsewhere, the next step forward could completely revolutionise our gardening world.

For just around the corner ready to lay siege to the gardening market is COMPUTAPLANT – the fully robotised micro-circuit gardening system that totally obviates the gardener himself; all that is required is a central computer terminal from which the entire garden can be controlled.

By inputting a few simple instructions, the gardener can call up Old Adam, the robot gardener, who is fully equipped to deal with all normal gardening functions. The gardener sits at his VDU screen and can tend the garden in a matter of seconds by keying in his requirements. The terminal does not even need to be near the garden; it is possible for a gardener to supervise the management of his garden from several thousand miles away simply by telephoning his instructions via an adaptor.

Alternatively, he can hand the whole thing over to a management agency which, with full access to his programme files, can superintend any number of gardens simultaneously. Indeed, so remarkable is the system that, by pre-programming, the gardener can leave his garden on auto-control for several years without it coming to any harm or damage.

So far, early tests in Japan on the system have proved inconclusive. Old Adam proved less than reliable in extremely wet or damp conditions – rather like a real gardener, in fact – and was prone to attacks of frenzy, ripping the heads off plants, attacking the prize lobelia with the electric hedge-clippers, and destroying several suburbs of Mitsubishi with the laser hedge-clippers.

However, the Japanese manufacturer claims that a modified system, tried out on Bonsai gardens, has proved a great deal more successful, despite the extra micro-technology required.

The package needed costs at present some $2½ million for a single unit, which may put it beyond the means of the average non-Japanese gardener. However, with further development they hope to get the price down to about £49.50 within the next six months.

Also for the home gardener, COMPUTAPLANT offer a number of software packages of computer game simulations.

GARDEN WARS A war game adaptation for the gardener. Gardeners compete to keep weeds and pests at bay in their garden. A range of pests and diseases appear on the screen and, armed only with a kettle full of hot water and a spray-gun full of something rather sticky and nasty whose name no one can remember, the player must keep all the invaders at bay. Length of game at lowest skill level: 30–40 minutes.

WEEDO Similar to GARDEN WARS, only more advanced. Normal duration of the game: about 3½ seconds.

PLANT DEATH 2000 Gardener must re-stock entire garden without re-purchasing stock from garden centre or shop. The gardener has to avoid bankruptcy, divorce and general ridicule in the process.

WEEDMAN The gardener takes on the role of a weed in this particularly authentic game, and has to avoid all the efforts of the computer-gardener to get rid of him. This allows the gardener to see and experience life on the other side of the trowel. WEEDMAN II is a similar game, but in this version the weed is a triffid and the objective is completely to take over a small North European country.

GARDEN CENTRE A test of nerve and skill as the gardener has to negotiate his trolley through an ever narrowing range of garden centre shelving to reach the cash desk. Points are awarded for skill, dexterity, and the ability to avoid serious psychiatric disorders.

BIG LAWN The TV screen becomes a lawn, and the gardener must try and cut it before the rain begins. To make the job more difficult, the hover flex gets more and more entwined, and the mower itself breaks down ever more frequently. This program, modified, is used to train lawnmower manufacturers.

SHRUBBERY The gardener must identify and talk authoritatively for at least twenty minutes about shrubs that appear on the screen, without putting himself to sleep. The winner is invited to make an award-winning TV documentary.

XZ 194 Completely meaningless game based on the chemical labels of pesticide jars. There are no rules and no one really understands what it's all about – or indeed what on earth they're supposed to be doing. Very authentic. Keep out of the hands of children.

Gardening Update

State of Garden

INDOOR

GARDEN   38499494949494949494949494448272638844449444 (Large Fitting)

DETAILS AS FOLLOWS

JUST WAITING FOR IT

NEARLY THERE

HANG ON

BE THERE IN A TICK

HERE IT COMES .

PLANTS	1
DEAD PLANTS	37
PLANT GAINS	NIL
PLANT LOSSES	37
WHEELBARROWS	NIL
LAWNMOWERS	NIL
INDOOR GREENHOUSES	NIL

PLEASE KEY PRESTEL PAGE   1162662535343337728282.827633

FOR FURTHER DETAILS

BUM

OH WHAT A GIVEAWAY

PRESTEL

Gardening Update

State of Garden

GARDEN USER ZX 35272272783883838383838838883 (recurring)

DETAILS

WEEDS   18226626535353535

PLANTS   2

LAWNS   N.A.

GREENHOUSES

              KEYCARD   9072653434343442

ACTION

SEE PRESTEL PAGE   455638829902

OR IF CLOSED,PRESTEL PAGE 36454554748

OR PRESTEL PAGE 029282273363

ADDITIONAL NOTES TO USER

HADDOCK   97

PILCHARD   4

WOMBLES   1029837

NOTTINGHAM FOREST 4   MANCHESTER UNITED 2

GARDEN POND UPDATE

DETAILS

PONDWEED

GOLDFISH   SEE

PRESTEL PAGE 374646646455 SHARKS

PRESTEL PAGE 364747474746 DEEP SEA TRAWLING

PRESTEL PAGE 465586757473 ICEBERGS

PRESTEL PAGE 877162525555 NAVAL BATTLES

PRESTEL PAGE 877365335352 DEAD GOLDFISH

HINTS FOR GARDENERS

Page 3647555886969966

ANSWERS TO LAST WEEKS PROBLEMS

YES

NO

YES

NO

POSSIBLY

PROBABLY

WITH A HARPOON

ALTERNATE TUESDAYS

ONLY BETWEEN CONSENTING POLICE OFFICERS

NO,USE A FORK

IT IS NOT A CRIMINAL OFFENCE BUT DO CONSULT YOUR DOCTOR

NO

NO

NO

DEFINITELY NO

DEFINITELY NO. UNLESS SPECIFIED BY THE LAWNMOWER MANUFACTURER

YES

392 FOR 6 DECLARED

M'BUNGO

TONY JACKLIN

9 FILM LIST

G.I. Blues

A guitar-playing gunner with the American Army in West Germany falls for a cabaret dancer.

Routine star vehicle marking Elvis Presley's return from military service, but dangerously thin on genuine parts for plants. Presley's dominance of the script ruins what would otherwise have been an excellent vehicle on the problems of servicemen returning to America after military service.

w Edmund Beloin, Henry Garson.   d Norman Taurog.
ph Loyal Griggs, st Sambucos   rf Potentilla
qz Philadelphus   nb Cytissus   og Cotoneaster
mz Dogwood   zz Hedera

Planet of the Apes

[Nearly a good film because *planet* sounds like *plant* if you take the 'e' out.]
Astronauts caught in a time warp land on a planet which turns out to be Earth in the distant future when men have become beasts and the apes have taken over.

Not nearly as good as it would have been if men had become plants and had taken over. Nevertheless 'apes' is very similar to 'grapes' if you put 'gr' in front of the 'a'. Or indeed 'apples' if you put 'pl' in the middle of the word. In fact, had it been called 'Planet Of The Apples' or even 'Plant Of The Apples' (a film about apple trees), then it would have been a *very very* good film indeed!

Sequel: Beneath The Plant (*sic*) Of The Apes
        Escape From The Plant (*sic*) Of The Apes

Conquest Of The Plant (*sic*) Of The Apricots (*sic*)
Battle For The Plant (*sic*) Of The Tinned Strawberries

The Bridge over the River Kwai

British P.O.W.s in Burma are employed by the Japs to build a bridge. Meanwhile British and American agents seek to destroy it. Ironic adventure epic with many fine moments but too many centres of interest and not nearly enough floral contributions. Many of the exotic Asian plants are misused by the power of a distinguished performance by Alec Guinness who attempts to save the bridge he has built but completely neglects the flowers.

Starring Alec Guinness, Jack Hawkins, William Holden, some foreign flowers, André Morell.

'Gripping Second World War movie spoilt by a failure to fully exploit the vegetable to the full' – *Gardening Times*

Awarded Oscars for best picture, best script, best orchids, best weeds, best grass, best gardener, best gardener's boy, best key gardener, best gardener's gardener, best trowel.

Brief Encounter

A suburban housewife on her weekly shopping visit develops a love affair with a local doctor. Very few flowers indeed, especially in the railway station scenes. Some flowers in vases. Also in the park. Very few exotic shrubs.

With Celia Johnson, Trevor Howard, Stanley Holloway, Joyce Carey, Cyril Raymond, and no flowers.

'A pleasure to watch as a well-developed piece, but where oh where were all the flowers' – *Amateur Gardener*

'Polished as this film is one cannot help but wonder why the director so obviously avoided flowers in the central roles' – *Gardeners Weekly*

The Sound of Music

Slightly muted, very handsome version of an enjoyably old-fashioned stage musical with splendid tunes. Completely made for this reviewer by one whole song entirely about a flower – 'Edelweiss' – based on the German flower of the same name. Also, there is another song with the word 'snowdrop', which is a type of flower. And there's another song about goats, which eat grass!

10 GARDENERS' PROBLEM PAGE

Q. *Last year I successfully rooted four pelargonium cuttings early in the season. Although they looked very healthy they have never flowered. Have you an explanation for this?*

A. Many men find it very difficult to respond after a traumatic experience like this. Remember to wear rubber gloves especially if either of your boyfriends suggests it. Do consult your doctor and tell him about the rabbit.

Q. *Several areas of my garden need clearing up, and as I am a dahlia lover I would like to fill them with a variety of dahlias. As tubers are so expensive, would it be possible to raise a selection of tall and dwarf ones from seed? Will they flower this year?*

A. It is remarkable how many people ask this question, and the answer in each case is quite simple: Who knows? I certainly don't. Neither does anyone else. And neither does anyone else, either. Do write and let us know how you get on. A photograph would be appreciated.

Q. *For several years I have tried raising zinnias in my greenhouse and then planting them out in my flower borders. The results have been disappointing. What is the secret of growing good plants?*

A. The secret of growing good plants is being a good gardener. If you are a good gardener, you should find it quite easy to grow good plants. If on the other hand you're not such a good gardener, then you will probably find that the plants you grow aren't nearly so good. It is as simple as that. If you want better plants, then the secret is to become a better gardener. Don't forget to include his foot-size on the application form and do remember to use a recognised preparatory cream when inserting the altimeter. If the problem persists, consult a qualified fishmonger.

Q. *Why did the pansies I planted out last summer turn yellow and die off rapidly?*

A. We are sending you a special booklet entitled 'Why my pansies turned yellow and died off rapidly'. It deals sympathetically with this very awkward and sensitive personal problem. We hope this will answer your needs.

Q. *I am sending you leaves off my parsnips. Could you please identify what is wrong. I have the same problem on my turnips and cauliflowers although not as bad.*

A. Basically, the problem both you and your partner are suffering from is a very serious one. Sending leaves through the post to strange people you have never met before is a disease, and the sooner people realise it the better. Consult a doctor. Or better still, emigrate to Canada. This sort of thing is probably quite normal over there. If not, they're only Canadians so it doesn't really matter if it upsets them.

Q. *How big can tomatoes grow? With so many varieties on the market, how can I tell what the fruit will be like?*

A. Well, as a broad guide, it is unlikely any fruit you grow will be larger than a medium-sized double-decker bus. Equally, it is not likely to be smaller than the top of a pin head. This should answer your problem. To find out what the fruit will be like you should ask someone who knows and they will tell you.

Q. *Although it only affects the odd Brussels sprout or cauliflower, my soil contains club root spores. How can I treat it?*

A. Frankly, you would be ill advised to treat the spores in any way. Generally speaking, it is a bad idea to treat spores, as they will begin to like it and may well expect you to keep on treating them in future. In particular you should not treat them by buying them presents and taking them to the pictures. The best thing to do is to ignore them completely. With any luck they should grow bored and may very well go elsewhere for their treats.

Q. *Last summer a white powdery mildew developed on the leaves of my marrows, just after the plants started flowering. I don't think it affected the crop, but it did look unsightly.*

A. The best way to get rid of mildew like this is by using some very strong words. We usually stand in front of our plants and say things like 'Go away, Mildew' and 'Push off, you nasty Mildew'. Honestly, that's what we do. Try and do this in a prominent position where the neighbours can see you. No, really, go on, that's what we always do.

Q. *How tall should I let my broad beans grow before I pinch out the tips?*

A. I'm sorry, but the doctor does not enter into personal correspondence. Your local Family Adviser clinic may be able to give assistance, or a good chiropodist might help. On no account attempt to remove both pairs of underpants without first ensuring the safety equipment is in place (see Twigs).

Q. *Circumstances have forced me to give up a very beautiful garden. Now all I have is a quite large open-aspect balcony. Is there any way I can keep myself supplied with fresh salads during the summer?*

A. Yes, buy them from a greengrocer.

Q. *What is the best way of looking after my plumbago?*

A. Extremely carefully.

Q. *I am interested in growing celosias as pot plants for greenhouse display this summer. Which would be the best variety to choose? It is very difficult to get them to flower. Any advice on raising celosias and caring for them would be appreciated.*

A. Well, the panel have spent a great deal of time considering your very interesting question and, basically and as a rough guide, we would do the same as you. Whatever you would do, then we would do it too. Ask yourself very carefully what you yourself would do under the circumstances and you can be pretty certain that we'd do the same. We hope that gives you everything you need to know.

P.S. if you're the same person who wrote to us about your streptocarpus, then the advice is, do exactly what you would do yourself, as we feel that is what we would do as well.

Q. *I have ordered a greenhouse and would like to know the best place to site it in my garden.*

A. Well, perhaps the best way to answer your question is to indicate where not to site it. 1) For a start, do not site it on top of the garage roof. Apart from spoiling the appearance of your house, it is likely to be extremely difficult to get at without a stepladder. 2) Another place not to site the greenhouse is on top of an existing greenhouse. Two greenhouses, one on top of the other, are notoriously unpopular and will only irritate and annoy any neighbours who have to look at it. 3) Do not put your greenhouse across a driveway or access path. It is particularly irritating not to be able to put the car into the garage at night because a greenhouse is in the way. There is also the danger that you might forget and drive the car through the greenhouse without realising what you are doing till it is too late. 4) Finally, be careful not to put the greenhouse on land that doesn't belong to you . . . especially if the land you choose suffers from one of the previously mentioned faults. There can be few more annoying things than coming home to find someone has put a greenhouse on your garage roof or across your driveway or on top of your existing greenhouse.

Finally, never put a greenhouse on a two-inch window ledge without warning the people who live below what you are doing.

Q. *For the past two years I have been growing tomatoes in gro-bags. But each mid-September, a problem develops. About six inches of each stem turns brown, and when cut they are hollow and powdery. What can I do to prevent this from happening again this season?*

A. Have you considered spicing up your love life by wearing exotic underwear or a flimsy nightie? Remember, you can do a lot with make-up, and bra and panties can be livened up for just a few pounds. The same goes for your wife, too.

Q. *Is it necessary for me to use arching to train and bring into fruit my maiden 'Victoria' plum?*

A. Remember that training methods are vital for young plants like the plum. Consult a qualified plumber for all your plum problems.

Q. *What is wrong with my mature cherry tree? The leaves on the new growth have curled up; also the bark is splitting and resin seeping out.*

A. Ugh! What a horrible mess! Cut back the infected foliage. Cut back the uninfected foliage. In fact, cut the whole thing off completely and throw it away. Cover the whole area where it used to be with concrete and buy a nice rustic bench to go on it.

Q. *The eating apple I have grown from a pip is rather spindly. What do I do next?*

A. Throw it away. There is absolutely no point in eating an apple like that. You won't enjoy it and it will only make you ill. Buy a chocolate bar instead if you still feel hungry.

Q. *This year my crop of 'Bramley' apples had brown spots right through to the core. What could have caused this and how can I prevent it?*

A. It's difficult to be certain without seeing the fruit, but we suspect fish in the atmosphere. Too many fish in the atmosphere frequently makes apples turn brown. There is not a great deal you can do to stop this occurring. Incidentally, fish in the atmosphere is often a problem with gardens grown beneath the surface of the sea.

Q. *How do I prune and trim Prunus cerasifera 'Altropurpurea' for a flowering hedge?*

A. The procedure for trimming Prunus cerasifera 'Altropurpurea' is to buy a book on the subject, read the book, then follow the instructions given in the book. This should trim the plant quite satisfactorily.

Q. *My seven-year-old yucca has flowered for the first time. Do I let the stem die back and will it flower again this year?*

A. Yes, and no. Though not necessarily in that order.

Q. *Is there an effective and practical treatment for lichens growing on shrubs, particularly deciduous and evergreen azaleas?*

A. Yes, the practical treatment for lichens growing on shrubs is to remove the lichens and then the plants will be all right. The trick lies in how you remove the lichens. Good luck and do let us know how you get on.

Q. *Could you suggest an evergreen hedge for a trough of soil two to three feet wide and 18 inches deep, between two drives? Ideally, we would like a conifer hedge about 3–4 feet high.*

A. No.

Q. *A friend tells me that gypsum can be sprinkled on the soil to help break it up. Is this true?*

A. Why not ask your friend? He seems to know all about it, doesn't he? If he's so clever, why come running to us to sort your problems out? Next time ask your friend to do your dirty work if he's so bloody clever. And do let us know how you get on. Smartarse.

Q. *Would leaf mould make as good a mulch as peat for my acid loam soil? I ask because though I often hear peat recommended I have an excellent supply of very well rotted leaf mould from my established wood of oak, sycamore and elm. Holly also grows in parts of the wood – are its leaves detrimental when well rotted?*

A. Yes, definitely. Leaf mould is definitely as good as peat. In fact, it's better. Because leaf mould is, er, a lot more, mouldy, er, and peat isn't. Therefore, it is. Er, I would say that compared to peat, leaf mould is better. Except when perhaps it isn't quite as good, in which case it's not better. But one way or the other, it's probably a lot more useful than something else that isn't as useful. Definitely. Er, that should do, shouldn't it?

Q. *My husband has been seeing another woman and though he now tells me it is all over I still can't trust him. Should I forgive and* *forget? Or do you think it is right for me to mistrust him still? We have a wonderful sex life and he has got an extremely large sexual organ.*

A. We suspect that your onions have become infected with bacterial soft rot. Too much nitrogenous manure, feeding too late in the season and poor drainage are also contributory factors. Grow your onions as hard as possible this year, check drainage and improve it as necessary. Then ripen the bulbs thoroughly.